Travelling in Women's History with Michèle Roberts's Novels

M. Soraya García-Sánchez

Travelling in Women's History with Michèle Roberts's Novels

Literature, Language and Culture

PETER LANG
Bern·Berlin · Bruxelles · Frankfurt am Main·New York·Oxford·Wien

Bibliographic information published by Die Deutsche Nationalbibliothek
Die Deutsche Nationalbibliothek lists this publication in the Deutsche Nationalbibliografie;
detailed bibliographic data is available on the Internet at <http://dnb.d-nb.de>.

British Library and Library of Congress Cataloguing-in-Publication Data:
A catalogue record for this book is available from *The British Library*, Great Britain.

Library of Congress Cataloging-in-Publication Data

García-Sánchez, M. Soraya (Maria Soraya), 1975-
Travelling in women's history with Michèle Roberts's novels : literature, language and culture /
M. Soraya García-Sánchez.
  p. cm.
Includes bibliographical references and index.
ISBN 978-3-0343-0627-0
1. Roberts, Michèle–Criticism and interpretation. 2. Feminist fiction, English–History
and criticism. 3. Feminism in literature. 4. Feminism and literature–Great Britain–History–
20th century. I. Title.
PR6068.O155Z68 2011
823'.914–dc22
            2011006110

Cover design: Thomas Jaberg, Peter Lang AG

ISBN Peter Lang Publishing Group 978-3-0343-0627-0
ISBN Universidad de las Palmas de Gran Canaria 978-84-92777-68-6

© Peter Lang AG, International Academic Publishers, Bern 2011
Hochfeldstrasse 32, CH-3012 Bern, Switzerland
info@peterlang.com, www.peterlang.com, www.peterlang.net

All rights reserved.
All parts of this publication are protected by copyright.
Any utilisation outside the strict limits of the copyright law, without the permission of
the publisher, is forbidden and liable to prosecution.
This applies in particular to reproductions, translations, microfilming, and storage and
processing in electronic retrieval systems.

Contents

Acknowledgments 7
Foreword by María del Carmen Martín Santana 9
Introduction 11

PART A
Michèle Roberts, the novelist 19

    Michèle Roberts's background 20
    Michèle Roberts and writing novels 24
    Pastiche and the concept of *L'écriture féminine*
    in Michèle Roberts 30
    Feminism: women's history 38
    Michèle Roberts's heroines 45
    Michèle Roberts's protagonists and their relationship
    with mothers: the conscious femininity 53
    Sex and religion in Michèle Roberts's novels 66
    Body and language in Michèle Roberts's work 80

PART B
Michèle Roberts, the memoirist 93

    Michèle Roberts's memoir: walking as a woman *flâneur* 95
    Paper Houses: a woman's fictional memoir 102
    Michèle Roberts's personal and public *Paper Houses* 106
    The structure of Roberts's memoir: locations,
    anecdotes and form 120
    History and culture in London: the 1970s and 1980s 130
    Index: writers and historical women
    mentioned in *Paper Houses* 136

PART C
Talking with Michèle Roberts: two interviews in 2003 and 2010 139

    Talking about women, history and writing
    with Michèle Roberts 139
    A conversation with Michèle Roberts about novels,
    history and autobiography 154

Conclusions 165
Bibliography 169

Acknowledgements

I started this book after having submitted my doctoral thesis to the Universidad de Las Palmas de Gran Canaria in 2004. Some chapters have been rewritten here after having been published in different academic journals. Acknowledgement is made to the following journals for permission to reuse the following articles in this book. 'Talking about Women, History and Writing with Michèle Roberts' was first published in *Atlantis: Revista de la Asociación Española de Estudios Anglo-Americanos* 27.2 (December 2005): 137-147. 'A Conversation with Michèle Roberts about Novels, History and Autobiography' first appeared in the *Journal of International Women's Studies* 12.1 (January 2011).

As for financial help, I sincerely wish to acknowledge the Agencia Canaria de Investigación, Innovación y Sociedad de la Información (ACIISI) for a travel research grant while I stayed at the Institute of English Studies at the University of London in 2010. Thanks to the Institute of English Studies for welcoming and offering me inspirational and physical space, and access to the University of London Library while I was a visiting Research Fellow. I am also committed to the Universidad de Las Palmas de Gran Canaria, and especially to the Servicio de Publicaciones and Difusión Científica, and to Peter Lang Publications for making this book possible. Thank you both for your support and for being such a wonderful, qualified team.

Fortunately, I have a wonderful family and there are many relatives, colleagues and friends I would like to publicly thank for their encouragement and confidence while this book was written and edited. They have contributed to develop this project in direct and indirect ways. I am also indebted to Mª del Carmen Martín Santana for offering me prudent and mature advice, and for her friendship. My thanks also go to Mª Teresa Medina, Antony Pérez, together with Pino Ramírez, Manolo Septiem, Susana Chaves and Dan Gibbs for their constant encouragement and hospitality while I was living in London, Australia and Gran Canaria. Finally, although not least, I want to fully acknowledge my gratitude to my husband for his loving support during the process of this work. This book is dedicated to him.

Foreword by María del Carmen Martín Santana

Hoy llega a mis manos el libro de M. Soraya García-Sánchez *Travelling in Women's History with Michèle Roberts's Novels: Literature, Language and Culture*, y este hecho me alegra por varias razones. La primera, porque Soraya es una persona a la que estimo sobremanera. La segunda, porque se trata de un volumen de contenido novedoso y fruto de un trabajo arduo. Y, la tercera, porque el documento es un regalo para la comunidad universitaria y para el público en general.

He conocido a Soraya a través de los años, ella haciéndose mayor y yo madura, y sólo tengo palabras de admiración por el esfuerzo que ha llevado a cabo. Como estudiante de Filología Inglesa se le veían tesón y entusiasmo a raudales, cualidades que promovieron que deseara continuar con su carrera investigadora. Así se acercó a mí, hace ya algunos años, y las dos nos dispusimos a navegar esas aguas. La travesía no siempre ha sido fácil, pero la firme disposición de aquella un día mi doctoranda logró salvar todos los escollos que aparecieron en el horizonte. Ella es hoy no sólo una gran amiga, sino también una compañera de profesión eficiente y querida por sus estudiantes y colegas, entre los cuales me cuento.

El libro, ya desde su título mismo, habla de variadas parcelas de la vida. Viajar, literatura, lengua, cultura… Y todas ellas sugieren riqueza de contenidos y crecimiento personal. Eso es lo que puede sustraerse de su lectura. No sólo nos encontramos ante una biografía, hacemos asimismo frente a un manifiesto de energía vibrante y amor por la existencia, la de la autora y, por ende, por la de todas las mujeres, que nos vemos reflejadas en los personajes y las disecciones que de ellos hace la Dra. García-Sánchez. La primera parte nos acerca a esta narradora de sueños que es Michèle Roberts. La segunda ahonda en su obra autobiográfica con todo lujo de detalles. Y todo ello se ve enriquecido, en la tercera parte, con las entrevistas que la Dra.

García-Sánchez ha podido realizarle a través de los años, un tiempo del que se ha valido para conocer a la novelista a fondo. Las conclusiones no dejan sombra de duda del exhaustivo trabajo realizado, y la bibliografía da fe de la búsqueda incesante de material con el cual tejer la urdimbre de este vasto documento que, por suerte para los lectores, hoy ve la luz.

Por todo lo anteriormente expuesto, puedo afirmar que me visto deleitada por la lectura que hoy llega a mis manos, fruto de una semilla que yo misma planté con la autora y que he visto crecer con y junto a ella. Se trata de un tomo valioso para todos los que tenemos que ver con la Universidad y, cómo no, para los que disfrutan con lecturas enriquecedoras e interesantes. Sólo me resta felicitar a la Dra. García-Sánchez por un trabajo impecable, y desear que las personas que se acerquen a este ejemplar puedan disfrutar de él tanto o más que yo. Mi más sincera enhorabuena, Soraya.

Mª del Carmen Martín Santana,
Universidad de Las Palmas de Gran Canaria

24 de enero de 2011

Introduction

I have had the extraordinary experience and pleasure of having met Michèle Roberts on different occasions in Maldon, London and Bath. Yet, when I first read some of her novels, *The Wild Girl*, *The Book of Mrs Noah* and *In the Red Kitchen* in one of the courses I was attending as part of my PhD studies, I felt haunted by her writing. Roberts is such a brilliant personality and a noteworthy influence on my professional career. With Roberts, I have learnt not only about women's studies and feminism but also about language and culture as well. Being an outsider and a foreign language speaker, I have been able to understand and share what this other world is about with *Paper Houses: A Memoir of the '70s and Beyond* (2007). Roberts's memoir intertwines with Roberts's novels as in both written forms there is a protagonist who finally tells her story for the very first time. The first person narrator in this true account is real but is also rescued from her past and reshaped at the time of writing this memoir.

I have also lived and strolled in London as a woman *flâneur*. The perspective of the 1970s depicted in Roberts's account, however, is that of an independent and feminist revolution for women. Today's London is not the same that London during the 1970s. Following Roberts's physical and literary steps has given me language. I have enjoyed analysing her fictional work and looking into her autobiography. Topics such as feminism, language, metaphor, action, body, Catholicism and sex, for instance, comprise Roberts's work. The world of feminism, together with the idea of western women writing their own texts are focal points while reading and studying Roberts's novels and *Paper Houses*.

Michèle Roberts is an Anglo-French woman, brought up Catholic and Protestant with two languages and cultures merging at the same time. Her work and her persona deal with the combination of opposites, replacing the correlative conjunction *or* with the coordinating conjunction *and*. Moreover, Roberts is a contemporary and feminist author who has published critical essays, twelve novels, poetry, a play and a variety of short stories. Her next novel will be published in 2011. By means of Roberts's work, and especially of her novels, I have been able to learn about historical women who have become new characters in her works of fiction. Mary Magdalene, Saint Teresa of Ávila. Mary Wollstonecraft, Charlotte Brontë are examples of real women who become heroines in Roberts's works of fiction. The practical novel has provided me with knowledge about women's writing, women's voices, femininity, masculinity, feminism, gender, society, Catholicism and theory, among others.

As a lecturer in English studies, I have always had passion for English speaking cultures, histories and traditions choosing what I enjoyed most and rejecting what I did not. Even when my much-loved husband goes to the bookshelves at libraries and bookshops, he checks on Michèle Roberts's work, just in case there is a new publication that I may not be aware of. 'She is always next to Nora Roberts,' he once said. I have become a woman with two parts of me, looking at the English and the Spanish worlds. In fact, both languages and cultural traditions differ but they also share essential human features dealing with men and women in history and society. I share with Roberts the influence of the Catholic religion and the impositions of the patriarchal society. Although we have both experienced different historical times and countries, I have discovered the feminist world by means of Roberts's novels and, consequently, by researching theoretical texts. That is the reason why I want to start this book in the first person narration. I want to participate in a woman's writing that connects body and language, as presented in Roberts's work. I feel that I need to state the connection between the identities of Roberts and mine because this book is the result of that bond. The combination of both voices, my own and more significantly Roberts's, forms this new book dedicated to Michèle Roberts's work of fiction, in the first section, and to her memoir, in the second section.

Travelling in Women's History with Michèle Roberts's Novels: Literature, Language and Culture is about Michèle Roberts's prolific production. She is an example of a woman's writing different to the traditional writing of men. I will be dealing with Roberts in order to explore that her novels offer a subversive revision of history and a recreation of women's writing. Roberts has been inspired by historical, mythological, religious and everyday women who have given form to her novels. In *Impossible Saints* Josephine, for instance, is inspired by Saint Teresa of Ávila. Roberts's Mary Magdalene plays the role of the controversial, historical Mary Magdalene in *The Wild Girl*. I will also analyse Roberts's most recent text, her autobiography, *Paper Houses: A Memoir of the '70s and Beyond*, which is a combination of past and present, individual and collective, man and woman, heterosexual and homosexual, private and public in search for Roberts's identity as a woman and as a writer in London. By means of her memory, her collection of handwritten diaries and some photos, Roberts tells us what she remembers of herself and of her previous years in London when the women's revolution was also taking place. However, it is important to highlight that this process of remembering is creative as it imagines a new identity based on memories and diaries. Roberts revisits her past by re-reading her notebooks and diaries and by remembering her experiences as a young rambler from London. Roberts is both writer and protagonist of her memoir which is real and fictional at the same time.

Even though this book is presented as academic research that must be *serious* and formal, this writing does not separate feelings from theory. Although this text aims to be objective rather than subjective, I do not intend to hide my voice. My perceptions will connect with the theoretical part that comprises this project. It is by means of the analysis of Roberts's writing that I get to understand my passion for researching this contemporary feminist writer. Her essays, her poetry and more significantly, her novels have given me knowledge and the ability to reread her texts and to finally participate in her written explorations. Because Roberts deals with both body and language at the same time, and because it is only by means of continuity that this union can be asserted, I will not separate body and language in my writing either. Therefore I aim to explore Roberts's memoirs from a fictocritic perspective, as some Australian women writers have suggested. Criticism will occur from a story bound perspective. Moreover, I will look into the French phrase, *l'écriture féminine*, that has a fresh meaning every time a woman writes about her body and her language. The meaning of *woman* is portrayed in the text with a language that corresponds to the body. This is the only way I can be honest to my academic, political, social and feminist criticism. I will, accordingly, engage in a dialogical text with Roberts's writing by combining my reading analysis with my critical perspective and, by considering freedom, rules, theory and practice.

What I aim to explore in this book is the approach of women's writing in relation to Michèle Roberts's novels and memoir. It is also my purpose to look into the following terms as part of an identity that is being formed: travelling, *flâneur*, body, language, culture, feminism, autobiography and creative writing. I will particularly consider Roberts's novels and *Paper Houses* in order to examine her past and present inspirations, and her forms of writing. It will be paramount to study the importance of Roberts's heroines who are usually inspired by historical and religious women, as I mentioned before. In a way, I mean to travel with Roberts in order to discover her daily, social, political, personal, historical, fictional journeys in London. I aim to demonstrate that her personal story becomes a contribution to the general history.

As Jane Spencer has argued, 'If women's writing is important to the history of the novel, the novel is no less important to the history of women's search for a public voice' (viii). *Paper Houses* deals with a specific protagonist, Michèle Roberts, but at the same time, it is a personal contribution to history and to the history of women's writing in the 1970s and 1980s in London. Travelling is a vehicle of discovering not only the urban city but herself. Strolling in Roberts's mind will imply the union between present reconsiderations and past memories. Roberts revisited her past in order to meet her other identity: young Roberts. With Roberts's words, I will discover and will invite readers to see a different perspective: this contemporary woman's side and Michèle Roberts's perception. As readers, we are witnesses of her experiences and of her writing style. We participate in Roberts's personal story and, at the same time, we are able to remember historical events that the protagonist interprets and adapts to her own personal revolution. Language, literature and culture plus personal and historical situations construct this individual memoir of the 1970s and beyond. However, the function of words and the techniques depicted by this contemporary writer are focal points of this analysis in which the inside becomes predominant and, at the same time, equal to the outside. As the author stated, language came from deep inside her and as such she maintained it through her writing. Her inner voice corresponded to her outer tone:

> I trusted abstract reasoning less than thoughts that came out of my own experience in the world and from my own inner life. Poetry and novels arose from very deep down inside. They struggled up out of darkness and broke into the light. I trusted this process. I knew that language existed 'outside' in the world. (*Paper Houses:* 278)

This book is divided into three main chapters. Part A is dedicated to Michèle Roberts's life and works of fiction. The second chapter is devoted to the analysis of Michèle Roberts's memoir. Finally, the last section presents the two conversations I had with Michèle Roberts in London, the former about her novels and her writing in 2003 and the latter about her memoir and her writing in 2010.

Part A will look into the work of the feminist writer and the similarities and differences between her novels. I will observe how writing is a means of expression that allows Roberts's heroines to reflect upon their bodies which become free of restrictions in this writer's accounts. In this regard, I will focus on Roberts's rewriting of historical and biblical texts in her novels to provide her protagonists, who are usually historical and mythological women, with a voice and language. Interpretation is thus an important tool in this writer's work. Intertextuality and writing will be a subtopic devoted to Roberts's religion and inspiration at the time of shaping her novels. Roberts, who actively belongs to the feminist movement by revising stories of women in different historical contexts, rewrites stories in order to deconstruct and demystify women. Once Roberts's heroines are deconstructed, they are created as protagonists of new stories that are portrayed in her books. These narrative accounts do not have to be always true but they must portray the imagination and perception of the protagonists and their connection with life writing. Truth is so to Roberts's mind. Roberts's heroines will explore their inner and outer standpoints by writing their selves in the text.

Part B is especially dedicated to Michèle Roberts's memoir, *Paper Houses: A Memoir of the '70s and Beyond*. I will be exploring the writing of a personal account from the female *flâneur*'s perspective. This section will be devoted to the analysis of this fictional memoir. I will look at the similarities and differences between Roberts's novels and her memoir at the time of shaping the text. The protagonist of this personal and historical account will be both writer and heroine. Equally, I aim to analyse the notion of the female *flâneur* who strolls about the city of London to observe its streets by herself. This journey will transform Roberts's identity, expressed usually in personal and public terms. Michèle Roberts will construct her own personality by dealing with both personal and political issues. In this sense, a brief analysis of the structure of the memoir will be developed by looking at its content and form as two characteristics that grow together in Roberts's work. A study devoted to Roberts's history and culture during the 1970s and 1980s in London will conclude this second part.

Part C will conclude this analysis by presenting two conversations I had with Michèle Roberts first, in 2003 and recently, in August 2010. The first interview focused on Michèle Roberts's novels while the second conversation addressed the connection between fiction and autobiography, especially with regard to *Paper Houses*.

Travelling in Women's History with Michèle Roberts: Literature, Language and Culture is therefore a journey through the fictional and autobiographical work of Michèle Roberts. This manuscript travels through Roberts's literary production as a woman writer who explores different writing techniques. Not only literature, language and culture are considered in this expedition but also feminism, history and storytelling. Fictional and historical heroines are depicted in different locations and periods of time in order that they can tell their own stories. Roberts's heroines will address the importance of dealing with content and form or, in other words, with body and language. As a devoted reader of Roberts's literary work, I hope that you enjoy travelling in this journey of discovery, reading and writing.

PART A

Michèle Roberts, the novelist

This first chapter will analyse the novel as a literary genre. The novel has been the preferred and more exploited written form chosen by women writers such as Michèle Roberts or Charlotte Brontë, for instance. The nineteenth century was a remarkable time for the beginning of the woman novelist. It is by means of initial readings that Roberts starts rewriting and reinterpreting her historical protagonists' lives. At the Bath Literature Festival in 2005, Roberts stressed that 'factorial information can become myth at the same time.' Based on the argument of this quote, Roberts not only looks into real facts to create a fictional text but an autobiographical text can also take the shape of a novel as it will be demonstrated with *Paper Houses*. Fact and fiction are linked in Roberts's work. Lucasta Miller has also suggested that biographical texts, inspired by Charlotte Brontë, have similar characteristics typical of a work of fiction:

> All life-writing (as Virginia Woolf called it) is a paradoxical process whereby the fragmentary business of lived experience is moulded into a formal literary structure and given an artificial sense of direction. Etymologically, even the word "biography" – life-writing – is an oxymoron. At some level, all biographers borrow some of their narrative techniques from fictional storytelling. (Miller 64)

Likewise, I will also deal with *pastiche* and *l'écriture féminine* as forms that shape Roberts's style. The writer participates in different explorations when writing her works of fiction. Roberts highlights the connection between women's body and the text. There is not language if it is separated from its body. In this line, *pastiche* is also used by the feminist writer as a technique that combines short stories of women in order that they complete a new text, a unit. The Italian term derives from the culinary context in which leftovers are used to create a new meal on the following day. *L'écriture féminine* and *pastiche* will be paramount techniques when dealing with Roberts's novels. It will be demonstrated that different voices of women tell their stories in order to form a singular and multiple-voiced text. The story of a particular woman will have a connection with the stories of women in a community.

Feminism and its connection with women's history and with women's studies will be another section to consider in this first chapter A. In Roberts's production, feminism and women's history are intertwined as both perspectives have cultured the feminist writer. By exploring Michèle Roberts's novels, I will study the parallelism shared by Roberts's heroines, especially with regard to their relation with their mothers. Likewise, I will devote a few pages to *The Wild Girl* as a novel that portrays the heroine Mary Magdalene as a celebrated woman of body and language.

The association between the Catholic religion and sexuality is recurrent in Roberts's work. Roberts's heroines deal with the relation they have with their bodies, their sexuality and their spirituality. I will demonstrate that Roberts's protagonists will need to write their own texts in order to create a space for themselves and their own identity. As in *Paper Houses*, many of Roberts's heroines were depicted in search for a space that belonged to them.

Michèle Roberts's background

Michèle Roberts is a contemporary, Anglo-French, feminist writer born in Hertfordshire, England in 1949. She was brought up bilingual and in a Catholic school. She was the daughter of a Protestant English father and a Catholic French mother. It has been by means of writing, rewriting, and the revision of histories that the writer has fought back against the values defended by the Catholic Church, although she has said on different occasions that the Church has given her language and metaphors. Roberts's personal upbringing, having a French Catholic mother and an English Protestant father has been influential in her writing. Roberts's English grandmother nurtured this feminist writer during her early years. Roberts has always considered her grandmother a great source of inspiration as she was the female figure who used to tell her stories that gave Roberts space for imagination and daydreaming. In this regard, Roberts's grandmother was less conflicttive than Roberts's mother. Roberts has declared that her mother was that authoritative figure who wanted to dominate her daughter according to the conditions dictated by the patriarchal society. Not only the mother and daughter relationship has been pinpointed in Roberts's novels but also her relationship with her father, and Roberts's desire to be accepted by her father, another figure that represents the dominant society.

Michèle Roberts completed her studies in Oxford where she read a Bachelor of Arts in English. It was during these years at university when Roberts started to be part of the Women's Liberation Movement. Michèle Roberts has not only been a feminist activist, but she has also carried out other professions such as a librarian in Bangkok, a cook, and a creative writing professor, to name a few. Although she lives between France and England, she has also lived in Thailand, Italy, and the USA.

Roberts has always fought back against authoritarianism and against Catholicism. It is by means of her novels that the feminist writer creates new women who are liberated from religious, social and political restrictions. In this line, there are many depictions of women's body and sexuality in Roberts's heroines. For Roberts, the female protagonist is rescued in order that she can verbally and sexually express herself. Roberts's heroines are usually triumphant before the Fathers of the Church. For that reason, Roberts subversively finishes her works of fiction with the binaries between good and bad women in novels such as *The Wild Girl*, for instance, in which being a woman is not only fully depicted and celebrated but also, sex with the man.

Michèle Roberts's literary production is quite varied. This contemporary author has written novels, short stories, poetry, articles and essays. Her first novel, *A Piece of the Night* (1978), was written when the author was 29 years old. It shows biographical data about the search for Roberts's identity and sexuality. *The Visitation* (1983), *The Wild Girl* (1984) and *The Book of Mrs Noah* (1987) are three novels that deal with biblical women. Roberts has been inspired by her position as a woman in the church. Roberts has rewritten religious women's stories. In the three works of fiction mentioned, we get to know the stories of Eve, Mary Magdalene and Mrs Noah. Roberts is more experimental in her writing with *In the Red Kitchen* (1990), a narrative that combines different times and the voices of the three main protagonists: Flora, Hattie and the pharaoh's daughter. *Daughters of the House* (1992) won the British prestigious WH Smith Literary Award in 1993. *Impossible Saints* (1997) and *Fair Exchange* (1999) are two novels inspired by religious or historical women, being Saint Teresa of Ávila Roberts's muse in the first narration and Mary Wollstonecraft in the latter. *The Looking Glass* (2000) is the novel set in Normandy just before First World War, in which Genevieve is alone in search for a home and the love of the poet Gérard. Charlotte Brontë's myth is revisited and rewritten in *The Mistressclass* (2003), a novel that combines the stories of the Brontë sisters and those of two writers and sisters living in contemporary London. The two stories intertwine to connect past and present. *Reader, I Married Him* (2005) is about Aurora, the woman who transforms her persona every time she gets married. Aurora becomes someone else every time she gets marries until she starts killing her husbands. Michèle Roberts's narrative is therefore not only varied but it is changing as I aim to demonstrate in the following pages.

The titles chosen by Michèle Roberts in her works of fiction are revealing. Just by scanning these titles, the reader can start imagining what the topics of Roberts's novels are. *The Wild Girl* or *Impossible Saints* refer to the woman who can express herself verbally and physically (sexually), even though that will imply fighting against the values imposed by society. On the one hand, Mary Magdalene is the girl who is not domesticated but wild. On the other hand, Josephine is the woman who cannot be a saint, as neither can the unnamed protagonists who intertwine their stories with that of Josephine's.

Likewise, *The Book of Mrs Noah* connects biblical texts but Roberts provides the message of a book that is created by an unknown woman, a woman without a first name. This creative, unknown woman is known by her husband's name. Roberts rewrites Noah's account by including the woman in the text. *The Visitation* is equally a text related to the origin of humankind. Roberts is inspired by Adam and Eve and the differences between the sexes. *In the Red Kitchen* and *Daughters of the House* depict domestic places that have been associated with women. The house is the place where women must be and the kitchen allows women to create food that can satisfy their family. These heroines are not only housewives but they are also daughters of the house. They follow their mothers' position in the care of the members of the family. On the other hand, the kitchen that Roberts describes in her novel is red as the blood that is in our bodies, and the blood of the woman's menstrual periods.

In the Red Kitchen can be connected to *Flesh and Blood* because both novels share the topic of death at the beginning of the narration. After having read *A Piece of the Night*, one can observe how Julie, the protagonist, acknowledges her conscious writing from her inside and from her darkness. Darkness is the heroine's unconscious and also, the liberal state for the protagonist to find her inner self. *Fair Exchange* and *The Looking Glass* are the titles that do not specify what the story may be about but once the plot of both novels is read, one can understand such titles. *The Mistressclass*, however, allows the reader to imagine a story of love and sex between a man and a woman that is either a lover or a children's instructor. These roles will be illustrated through Charlotte Brontë and present-day Catherine. In the following section, I will explore every one of Roberts's novels starting with the first work published and ending with the most recent publication.

Michèle Roberts and writing novels

> I write novels to understand the wordless images, spin a story around them that will lay them, like ghosts. Also to answer questions: can mothers truly love daughters? Does a woman belong in this world and is she allowed to have a house of her own? I realized only recently that all my novels feature homeless women, that novels are the paper houses I build, then inhabit.
>
> At the same time I write novels to explore the form, to find out just what it can do. Different each time. The content (those images, those nagging questions) shapes the form; only that form can demonstrate that content. Yes, form is content ... The language is what matters. It has, is, body. (Roe 171)

This section has been introduced with Michèle Roberts's arguments as I will deal with the writer's inspiration and intentions at the time of writing novels. As the author suggests, her writing is about what has not been said. Roberts has aimed to come back with unanswered questions concerning women. Her writing aims to find a space that makes her belong as a woman. This space is not just the domestic house set for her condition of being a woman but a paper house. Paper houses empower Roberts to freely think, write and be, as the title of her memoir suggests (see Part B for further reading). The house is the place where a woman can express herself and listen to her own voice. She is the passive woman who works in the house. The active man, on the contrary, is free to move around outside the house. While the woman may be active and free in her house, the man is active and free usually outside the house. The woman in the house not only does domestic chores but she also looks after her father, her brothers, her husband and her children. Roberts is affirmative when she considers that she shares with her protagonists not having a house for herself due to her gender difficulties. According to the patriarchal thought, the female body was not meant to express her self but to be submissive. This idea of a space of one's own first appeared with Virginia Woolf's argument in *A Room of Own's Own* (1929).

Michèle Roberts has revealed, on numerous occasions, that writers such as Virginia Woolf or Doris Lessing are some of the most influential writers in her work. However, today Roberts does not feel Doris Lessing's influence any more as it was more a maternal authority than an influence.[1] Roberts rejects any sign of authority in her writing and that is the reason why the omniscient narrator is not commonly used in her work. In *Paper Houses*, the author clearly defends this argument when she says that she always needed 'to revolt against those in power over me' (16). Roberts, together with Virginia Woolf has always advocated the notion of the woman writer who is capable of producing her own texts and of being recognised as a writer, without the need of devaluing her gender. For Roberts and Woolf, being a professional woman writer is a field they want to conquer. They have highlighted how significant is for a woman to be recognised as a writer who can be creative and artistically accepted as men have always had.

The opposing system for Roberts is the phallocentric structure that has diminished the condition of women and their reality in history. The passivity projected on women has been criticised by different feminists such as Luce Irigaray, Hélène Cixous or Elaine Showalter. With Roberts's novels, there is a contribution to another structure that is not conflictive anymore but it allows space for literary creative women. Virginia Woolf was one of the first feminist writers to suggest that women should have a space of their own that would allow them to be free of any limitations:

> But this freedom is only a beginning; the room is your own, but it is still bare. It has to refurnished; it has to be decorated; it has to be shared. How are you going to finish it, how are you going to decorate it? With whom are you going to share it, and upon what terms? These, I think are questions of the utmost importance and interest. For the first time in history you are able to ask them; for the first time you are able to decide for yourselves what the answers should be. (Woolf 9)

Michèle Roberts has maintained in different interviews that she has felt nearer to writers such as Virginia Woolf or Charlotte Brontë, for instance, than to contemporary feminist writers such as Angela Carter

---

1 García Sánchez, María Soraya. 'Talking about Women, History, and Writing with Michèle Roberts'. *Atlantis* 27.2 (December 2005): 137–47.

or Doris Lessing, who are also mentioned in *Paper Houses*: 'I feel much closer to Colette, Catherine Mansfield, Virginia Woolf, and actually to the nineteenth-century writers such as Charlotte Bronte, than I do to my immediate predecessors' (Galván 359-60). Roberts, however, has also remarked that Doris Lessing was also significant in her literary production. *The Golden Notebook* (1962) was the first literary work written by Lessing for women, and it is still today a paramount text in the women's studies arena. With Lessing's book and the readings of the nineteenth century writers, Roberts has discovered the novel from a different standpoint. The novel is now an organised text by a woman who is creating her own literary discourse and who is able to identify her own language with her body. This language and form would differ from the masculine literary discourse: 'What excited me was that to write about women you had to reinvent the novel, and think I really saw her doing that ... It was that sense of her saying that if you wanted to write about women's lives you had to find a different kind of novel' (Galván 363).

Roberts, like other writers, considers that a literary production is a combination of form and content. Both elements complement each other when a novel is created. Roberts's form and content correspond to language and body. Roberts's writing is that of a woman when her books are shaped. Her voice dictates the arguments of her body and mind. In this regard, Roberts's work can be seen as a representation of diversity in women's histories and stories. This variety aims to project the multiplicity of women in the world. There is not one or another personality but a plurality of many heroines seeking to discover and revisit the past, and therefore, to look into the archives written by women. Neither the structure of Roberts's texts nor her feminist protagonists will follow the masculine tradition imposed by the patriarchal society. Roberts is not dealing with a unique woman that is either good or bad but she may have multiple characteristics. Roberts's writing, like that projected by many other contemporary women, is just the opposite. It is dual and even plural. Roberts aims to intertwine feelings with theory, inner voice with outer voice, body with language when writing as a woman.

When dealing with Roberts's writing style, the unconscious condition is another characteristic to consider. Roberts's protagonists are, on numerous occasions, women who need darkness in order to liberate their minds. The unconscious is crucial for Roberts's heroines in order that they can write and express their internal voices. This darkness is necessary for the female characters as they feel free and able to produce in that psychological, liberated space. They produce what they feel and what they are and as such it is presented on paper. This healing and creative writing begins in the darkness in order to make the true expression of the female characters possible. Roberts allows her heroines to be able to establish an active role in literature. Many women used to be closed in their bedrooms in order to become free, independent, and lonely. Only in this solitary space could they express what they really felt as bodies with witty thoughts and feelings.

In the Red Kitchen is one of Roberts's novels that clearly depicts the unconscious world and creation by means of writing. In this work of fiction Michèle Roberts argues that darkness is imperative for her protagonists. Flora, the main character in the narrative, who will connect with different stories in the novel, shows in the following lines how darkness becomes her home and thus a liberating space for her:

> So darkness becomes a homely place breathing in and out, an enormous room in which to fly free, roam unconstricted, turn somersaults.
>
> Darkness has always been necessary to me. Now it is my one faithful companion. Walking at four a.m. as I so often do these days, I pull it around me as a comforter, and settle to continue writing this story of my life. For no reason except to please myself. (17-8)

The unconscious psyche of the protagonist, who is being liberated in her darkness, is what makes her write this story about herself and for herself. She does not need to please anyone else. It is by means of the writing form that this heroine finds her own personal place, free of authoritarian forms that will reduce her possibilities. As Erica Jong has pointed out, darkness is a necessary tool for the artist. The unconscious becomes necessary to create recognised and valued art: 'But the unconscious of an artist is her greatest treasure' (52).

It has already been said that Michèle Roberts's writing deals with revision of stories and situations already told but she offers a new and feminist viewpoint, the awareness of the historical, religious, mythological and everyday women. The fact of revising stories by means of writing makes the reader consider the idea of power as it has been the patriarchal society which has controlled history. With Roberts's works of fiction, stories by women are revised and rescued. Roberts has been inspired by historical characters that do now have a fictional role in the novels. Roberts's heroines become active women in her novels.

This history by women in the form of fiction rewritten by Michèle Roberts is totally linked to biography. It is by means of the characters' experiences that creativity is cherished so that Roberts's heroines deal with herstory instead of history. Sonia Villegas López in her article, 'Telling Women's Lives: Vision as Historical Revision in the Work of Michéle Roberts', points out that *Impossible Saints* is an example of a novel that combines fiction with biography in order to create a new story. Roberts has had to read and research about Saint Teresa of Ávila's life and written accounts in order to make this story up: 'Roberts initiates in this novel the task of transmitting those stories, which sometimes run parallel to the official biographies, in a process of 'recreation' of history' (2001: 185).

This experimental writing is a postmodern influence on the contemporary writer resulting in a 'fictional construct' (Villegas López 174). This new testimony is not based on true facts. This fresh story is not looking for historical documents that support Roberts's arguments. As an alternative, Roberts's works of fiction focus on the conscious approach of the protagonists' historical conditions which permits the postmodern writer to create a new, interpretative perspective in a subversive way. Roberts focuses on what history has not said. Postmodernism has been significantly used by women writers as it does not limit meanings but it allows more varied interpretations. Postmodernism also enables the writer and reader to consider unidentified understandings and merits of the historical women that are portrayed in Roberts's works of fiction: 'Not only that, there is a return in literature to famous historical figures of the past, though this time new sides to their character and their historical relevance revealed' (Villegas López 174).

Daughters of the House is another work of fiction inspired by Saint Thérèse of Lisieux. However, Roberts does not present Thérèse as the ideal woman that the patriarchal society has described but Thérèse is good and bad, passive and active. Roberts's Thérèse is closer to the reader. In the novel, Thérèse is a more reflective personality who looks inside her. As Roberts has declared, *Daughters of the House* is about 'anger, loss, terrific suffering, doubt, sex' (Galván 369). All the suffering that Thérèse experiences during her life is influenced by Catholicism. Roberts does not depict Thérèse as a horrible woman but as a woman who has been 'damaged by conventional piety' (Galván 369). The feminist writer has declared on numerous occasions that the Church makes you feel guilty of your own body and your sex, especially if you are a woman. Roberts argues that '[c]atholicism is not good for girls and women' (Galván 369).

The Wild Girl (1984) is another novel that shows the importance of starting to write from the unconscious, especially when the main protagonist is Mary Magdalene. In chapter twelve, Roberts describes how Mary Magdalene and other women are on the final judgement day. It is the man who is being judged for his harmful actions against women. The unconscious psyche liberates these women's minds and they call for the termination of the books written by men, as they do not tell the truth about women's inner feelings. Only women can narrate what they have experienced and felt. Women want to write about their bodies and their language. The books mentioned in *The Wild Girl* are historical books written only by men. Mary Magdalene and the other women want to rewrite history once those male books are in the fire: 'Let us burn all their libraries and burn their books. Let us destroy their lies and begin to tell the truth ... And so the contents of all the libraries in the world, from the whole history, were brought in and thrown on to a great pyre' (Roberts 173). There is continuity in Magdalene's argument as she aims to conclude with history in order that a rebirth of women's history is represented. The woman's body is portrayed by means of dreaming and looking into the liberated darkness: 'And I lost consciousness again ... I dreamed a fourth dream' (Roberts 174).

Some of Roberts's novels presented in this analysis question common characteristics of contemporary feminist literature. Yet Roberts also highlights the importance of reflecting upon women's writing. Roberts's connection between body and language is a paramount exploration in her fiction. This woman's writing engages in the plurality of meanings accepted by postmodernism. Roberts presents women's stories as personal and public history. Her heroines find their voice and the acknowledgement of various women identities. In her novels, Roberts will also show other topics sustained by feminism such as the interrelation between sexuality and religion, and the importance of words that represent the body of the writer. This women's writing that deals with body and language will be studied in the following section dedicated to the Italian term of *pastiche* and the French concept of *l'écriture féminine*.

Pastiche and the concept of *L'écriture féminine* in Michéle Roberts

It has already been conveyed that Michèle Roberts uses different techniques that allow a combination of stories to take place in order to create a novel. The Italian term *pastiche* was originally used to mix leftovers in order to create a new meal on the following day. Although *pastiche* was in the beginning applied to cooking, it can also be related to writing. Roberts uses *pastiche* in her novels. She collects different fragments of information that are initially depicted as independent pieces that are consequently united in a fresh story. With *pastiche*, it is possible to shape an innovative and subversive story of what has not been written before.

Pastiche has postmodern connotations. As a technique used in various novels by Roberts, *pastiche* is characterised by its relation to intertextuality. Hoesterey suggests that '[t]he Proustian pastiche is seen by Hollier as constituting the intertextual play that is literature, it is a dialogical mode of pastiche that becomes a major focus of cultural production in postmodernism' (9). On the other hand, *pastiche* refers to the capacity of creating by means of something that already exists. In the context of food, *pastiche* implies the making of a new meal with the leftovers of the previous day. In literature, *pastiche* takes place in a text that is formed as a unit but is, at the same time, composed of a collection of stories. *Pastiche* had its first connection with literature at the end of the eighteenth century: '[P]astiche in the visual arts suggests that the dissemination of the new concept and its application to literature did not occur until the last third of the eighteenth century' (Hoesterey 6). Likewise, Hoesterey argues that *pastiche* becomes part of a postmodern thought, an approach that deals with both reading and writing. The reading of texts initiates this process of the *pastiche* that is finally concluded by the creation of a critical and dialogical text: '[T]he pastiche is not so much writing but reading ... pastiche as the ideal form of creative critical activity' (Hoesterey 9). *Pastiche*, therefore, requires that the writer does both reading and writing in order to create a postmodern collective text.

This postmodern concept of the *pastiche* is present in Michèle Roberts's texts. As Roberts has already argued, *pastiche* and subversion are recurrent characteristics in her work. She needs to research the lives of her protagonists (Mary Magdalene, Mary Wollstonecraft, Teresa of Ávila) in order to invent and rewrite their stories which are usually shaped as novels. In the interview published in 2005, Roberts mentioned that *Flesh and Blood* (1994) required profound research of seventeenth century Italian culture. It was after the reading of historical documents that Roberts let her imagination go in order to create this work of fiction.

If we focus on the novel *The Looking Glass* (2000), we can observe that it is formed by nine episodes, starting with Genevieve's story which is alternated with the stories of four other women:

Millicent, Isabelle, Marie-Louise and Ivonne. These five female characters tell their individual stories but, at the same time, they all share a connection with the male protagonist, the poet. Every one of the protagonists falls in love with this intellectual figure even though he is described as ugly. In the same novel different events describing the relationships with Gerard take place. Likewise, the writer links not only the romantic stories of the female protagonists in relation to Gerard, but also, the feminist stories told by women. Roberts has highlighted the importance of these women's feelings which are portrayed on paper, especially when they have sexual relationships. Although the protagonists are limited to express their bodies by the patriarchal society, they experience sex and love and such it is written on paper. *The Looking Glass* forms a unit composed of all these different voices that move around a man, the language figure. The male poet represents the literary being that has had the freedom of speaking and writing while the woman has been silenced verbally and physically. By means of writing these accounts, Roberts's protagonists are able to find their identity. They are now capable of expressing their bodies and their thoughts and therefore to liberate themselves. Roberts's heroines write their stories which have their own first names as the titles of the chapters.

In the following lines, it is possible to observe the intimate tone of every one of the protagonists. Roberts's female characters share common features. They are searching for their identities and they are protagonists and writers of their own accounts in *The Looking Glass*. The use of the first person narration is highly relevant in this novel. Biruté Ciplijauskaité has suggested that the *I* voice not only refers to the plural conscious identity of women in society but also to the individual conscience of every protagonist (20). Even though every narrative told is unique, these women are dealing with a collective women's sense of right and wrong. The initial words of every chapter together with their titles are presented below to highlight the intentional *I* voice of Roberts's heroines in *The Looking Glass*:

GENEVIEVE
This is the sea I miss most: the music of the dragging tide over the loose shingle ... (1).

MILLICENT
June 10th

To me the river seems alive, like an animal ... (96).

ISABELLE
Gérard liked to describe to me the baths he had visited in North Africa ... (167).

MARIE-LOUISE
This effort of trying to discover and collect my earliest memories of my uncle ... (225).

YVONNE
My mother used to declare how sorry she felt for Madame Colbert (255).

Genevieve, Millicent, Isabelle, Marie-Louise and Yvonne are presented as women who tell their independent stories in *The Looking Glass*. They narrate their personal accounts in order to find their identities. Although these heroines do not get to know each other, they are linked in the story by the male poet. The five protagonists have fallen in love with Gérard. This same technique was already applied by Virginia Woolf in *Mrs Dalloway*. Edward Bishop suggests that Woolf's protagonists are linked by images and emancipated experiences that are expressed by means of their consciousness: 'Critics have noted how the characters are linked by 'collective images', and further how these characters seem to be not so much connected with each other as absorbed by the narrating consciousness which distils and renders their experience' (49).

Impossible Saints (1997) has a similar structure to that of *The Looking Glass*. Different stories alternate with Josephine's account. Josephine is the fictional character inspired by Saint Teresa of Ávila but Roberts's heroine is not Teresa as she suggests in the author's note that introduces the novel. The beginning and the end of this work of fiction are dedicated to The Golden House, a place that collects women saints' bodies such as Josephine's. In The Golden House, the body parts remain as expositions. Then the story of Josephine is alternated with other women's stories. These eleven women are everyday women whose accounts are presented in the text with the purpose of making them recognised. Roberts questions the conditions of these other women who are, like Josephine, impossible to become saints for the Catholic Church. For Roberts, the heroines of *Impossible Saints* are fully saints in this creative composition. The *pastiche* technique, mentioned before, is accordingly adopted by Roberts in order to mix different women's voices that shape a work of fiction which deals with more personal histories of women.

In a similar way, Roberts does combine not only four different women's voices but three different periods of time in *In the Red Kitchen* (1990). This fantasy piece combines the story of Hattie, the daughter of a pharaoh in old Egypt with nineteenth century Flora and the contemporary woman from London. During her time, pharaohs would be eternal and become gods after having died. Hattie aims to follow her father's actions to become immortal. In this regard, Hattie is the character that survived numerous periods of time and she will connect with Flora and the woman from London. Hattie will unite various periods of history and three women's stories in the same book: 'I have done what no woman has dared to do before me: I have named myself Pharaoh of Egypt. Power over all this land while I am on earth, sole power; I, only I; and life everlasting amongst the gods when I die. I am man, I am Pharaoh, and I shall rule' (100).

Daughters of the House (1992) is another novel that develops the *pastiche* technique. It is by means of Thérèse's and Léonie's voices that the two stories are written to compose this work of fiction. As the title of the novel suggests, the chapters that form this book are connected with objects of the house such as the wall, the recipe book or the alarm clock. Every object will be significant to the story told by the protagonists. All these elements of the domestic place introduce every chapter created by the protagonists of the novel. The heroines will go backwards and forwards to tell their stories. Present and past events will be in a constant dialogue. Thérèse and Léonie will be inside and outside the house to remember and reflect on the experiences they both shared in the same residence. The objects of the house gain importance in the story and they function as connectors of the protagonists' accounts. The house, the interior, is the place of these women and thus, the best location to tell their stories. Thérèse's and Léonie's past is rescued and revisited so that they can write personal and public stories:

> When she was little, Léonie was fascinated by the family photographs hung above the bureau in the main *salon*. On to thick grey paper were stuck the pictures that composed Antoinette's view of the present and the past. (27)
>
> Léonie's birthday was a week after Thérèse's, in mid July, just before she and Madeleine set off for their summer holidays with the family in France. (34)
>
> When she married Louis, Antoinette changed the house a bit, to modernize it. She had two bathrooms put it, and she had a dressing-room built, next to her bedroom. This was a sort of passage, short, lined with cupboards. (60)

In the same light, *Fair Exchange* (1999) reveals the story of Louise Daudry who needs to revisit her past before she can start writing her account. Although this is the character that introduces and concludes the novel, other heroines also participate in the narration of their own stories. In this novel, not only are flashbacks used but the protagonists move in a variety of spaces that are finally integrated to shape the text. Because in the epilogue of the novel Louise has finally told her account, she is positioned in a reflective present time. After having told her personal story, which at the same time evokes other women's stories, Louise gets better from her illness. It is precisely tomorrow, a future reference for changes, when Louise will be able to start a new life and a new story. Now that she has started to tell stories, she is urged to continue. Louise's listener is, significantly, a priest who has come to see her in such a fatal state. Louise has told her story in the form of a confession but the priest has fallen asleep. The priest represents the church that is not aware of women's needs, conditions and plural identities. Louise, however, has told her story straight away, without restrictions but looking into her unconscious:

> It was the wrong story for him. Not his style. But his coming to visit her had taught Louise one thing. Telling the story was as important as what was in it. She needed an audience, and tomorrow she would go out and find one and begin again. Perhaps this time she would tell François, and the children. (246)

To make her personal story public has relieved Louise who is now capable of expressing herself by means of using her own language. It does not matter if the account is boring for some like the priest. Louise has actively exposed her identity, her body and her language. Louise has told her story. She is not silenced anymore but active and creative. Although the priest being asleep shows his lack of interest for the story told, the protagonist has succeeded in expressing herself and in producing her own voice and her story.

This proposal of writing one's self in a text is extremely connected to the French feminist movement in which Hélène Cixous participated. She has made clear that writing, or to be more precise, women's writing or *l'écriture féminine*, must link to the body and to women writer's consciousness. In 'The Laugh of the Medusa', Cixous talks about writing by and for women. She also defends the thought that body and language should be combined when women writers contribute to literature and history:

> I shall speak about women's writing: about what it will do. Woman must write her self: must write about women and bring women to writing, from which they have been driven away as violently as from their bodies – for the same reasons, by the same law, with the same fatal goal. Woman must put herself into the text as into the world and into history – by her own movement. (245)

Michèle Roberts has also supported Cixous's argument. Roberts allows her protagonists to put their identities into their accounts. Roberts links the woman's body to writing as a woman. Being a woman is a celebration for these feminist writers. Roberts also writes about what has not been written, or at least, about some women who have not yet been heard: 'I want to put the body always into language. I was brought up in a tradition of reading and thinking at university that, in a sense, left the body out. It was all about your mind. That good writing didn't have a 'self' in it, didn't have an ego in it' (Richards 5).

When Roberts deals with language that expresses what women feel, think about and desire, the term *l'écriture féminine* comes to any contemporary feminist critic's mind. *L'écriture féminine* comprises not only the representation of the female body but also her sexuality and her written language. Because history has repressed women's sexual manifestations and desires, this feminine writing allows women to express their bodies and therefore their sexuality and their own language. Women link their bodies to forms of writing in order to express their identities. This bond is then represented in a women's writing that is different to that of men. Because women's bodies are different to men, women's writing differs from men's writing. Not only the mind but the body expressed women's language. *L'écriture féminine* provokes new opinions, new interpretations that are conveyed by various women's voices. With *l'écriture féminine*, Roberts offers her heroines the option of putting their identities into the written text.

The language used in Roberts's novels is direct and conscious. This language expresses what the female protagonists have in mind and what their bodies feel without considering any restrictive conditions. Hattie, one of the protagonists of *In the Red Kitchen* (1990), highlights the importance of writing as a way to acquire power. The word is for Hattie a way to become eternal: 'To write is to enter the mysterious powerful world of words, to partake of words' power, to make it work for me. To write is to deny the power of death, to triumph over it' (24).

Pastiche and *l'écriture féminine* are undoubtedly postmodern writing forms used by Michèle Roberts. The scholar Mary Klages establishes that women's writing is not contrary to men's writing or to the dominant forms of writing. Women's writing is simply indefinable. Women's writing is not objective but subjective, personal. The individual and public, female subject is able to express her inner self in written form. The woman must put her body into the text. There is a need for a subjective account that combines personal and public spheres. This women's writing suggests oral and written forms, order and chaos, necessary elements of Derrida's deconstruction.

By means of deconstruction, women writers can start creating new texts. One element will not be dominant over the other as this women's writing is about a balance between contraries that can coexist together. This *écriture féminine* aims to finish with opposites that are separated from each other. This women's language engages in a persistent harmony which implies multiple and differing elements: 'L'écriture feminine, like feminine speech, will not be objective/objectifiable; it will erase the divisions between speech and text, between order and chaos, between sense and nonsense. In this way, l'écriture feminine will be an inherently deconstructive language' (Cixous 5).

Undoubtedly, Michèle Roberts uses women's writing techniques such as *pastiche* and *l'écriture féminine* in her works of fiction. *Pastiche* is a postmodern technique that combines different stories in the same book. *Pastiche* is also a way to see intertextual references in a text. Different women's voices, who are telling their individual stories, are written in order to create a communal text. *L'écriture féminine* is about creating a writing form that is particular of women. Michèle Roberts's writing focuses on exposing women as human beings that are capable of expressing their bodies and minds in their texts. By linking language and body, women's writing is cherished and celebrated. This way of putting women's body into their texts emancipates the multiple identities of women who are not either one or the other but plural and many.

Feminism: women's history

Feminism is the term applied to the study of women in different contexts such as society, religion, language and sexuality. The definition of feminism has to do with emancipation of women and women's rights. In the case of contemporary writers such as Michèle

Roberts, feminism implies focusing on the heroine and studying her as a woman and as a professional. Feminism is also about rescuing the female protagonist and rediscovering the world of words by allowing the woman to develop unusual roles for her gender condition. This feminism is about women's personal experiences. Roberts's characters are active participants of feminism because they create their personal accounts. Roberts's feminism deals with stories of historical women's personal lives. It is also about the writing of women's stories and the history of women. Furthermore, Roberts's feminism is exploring equal opportunities at the time of writing as a woman. This feminist writer aims to find equality between men and women not only at personal and social levels but also professionally. As Joy Magezis argued, this feminist literature is about stories for and by women. Women writers such as Roberts create novels in which her women protagonists write their own texts. These women deal with social, economic, political, gender and sexual discrimination. Roberts's protagonists are inspired by real women who are looking into their inner selves to connect them with the outer and public world: 'Feminist literature is about women writing and that includes you. We all have our stories to tell and putting them down on paper helps to give us power. Often women start by telling their personal stories' (Magezis 89).

Feminism for Roberts is therefore a combination of different approaches. On the one hand, this writer is socio-political because Roberts maintains the importance of writing literature as a means to reform culture, society and history. Roberts rewrites stories of popular and historical contexts in order to give them a new, feminist voice. In *The Wild Girl*, for instance, Mary Magdalene is an active character who is triumphant from the limitations set in her socio-political context. Likewise, Roberts also deals with the socio-psychological approach as her heroines are awakening in her novels in order to find that feminine consciousness that will be part of their own individual identity. This second line of feminism aims for sisterhood:

> The Socio-Psychological Approach ... focuses on exploring the awakening feminine consciousness reflected in literature by and about women ... this critical approach has often stressed a psychological maturation not only through a

recognition of gender difference but also through a growing sense of 'sisterhood' with other women. (Fish)

The Visitation is an example of the socio-psychological approach. Helen, the main character, becomes conscious of her social and psychological background at the end of the novel. Helen identifies who she is in the concluding lines of the novel. Helen is able to write her own account from her within and thanks to other women's consciousness. Beth is presented in the novel as an image of sisterhood. Beth provides comfort to Helen and that encouragement improves Helen's personal and public awareness: 'She ached for mothering, the love that listening gives, the love that a woman now gives to her. Beth has nourished her in her need, before Helen knew what that need was' (172).

Finally, Roberts also participates in another type of feminism that deals with language. This feminist writer follows Hélène Cixous's argument about *l'écriture féminine* and defends the importance of a writing that belongs to women's bodies. For Roberts, women must put their bodies on paper and hunt for a new language that corresponds to the woman's interior:

> The Fe (Male) Approach of the French school of feminist criticism has stressed the subtle but essential participation of language in the patriarchal forces of society ... Some practitioners of this critical method also focus on defining the distinguishing qualities of *l'écriture féminine*. (Fish)

The Looking Glass (2000) is an example of a novel that highlights the importance of writing as a woman. Millicent, one of the protagonists, shows in the following lines her need of writing her personal diary so that she could maintain memories, feelings, thoughts and experiences. Her individual writing is paramount as it increases her confidence as an artist. This individual writing transforms the heroine into a free woman once she is writing her diary. By means of her personal account, Millicent writes what she wants, what she feels, just for the satisfaction of pleasing herself and no one else. Women's writing for their own sake is what Millicent portrays in the following lines. It is healing writing that looks deep inside its protagonists: 'That is where you come in, dear diary. Keeping a record of my experiences in France will give me something to do. All that I cannot utter in public, my criticisms particularly, I shall put down here. I'm writing this for myself, after all' (102).

Michèle Roberts has pointed out on several occasions the importance of feminism in her persona and in her professional writing. As she put it, feminism meant freedom for her. Feminism was not only a constructive home for Roberts but a way of expressing herself after having had several familiar conflicts for not adapting herself to the imposed norms. Feminism is, for Roberts, a way to share information and experiences with other men and women who want to find social justice:

> Feminism was home, and it did what home should do for you, it nurtured me and kicked me out into the world. I'm an old fashioned feminist – for me it's about loving other women and supporting other women in their struggles and it's very connected to movements in the world for social justice. (*BBC*)

Many other women in our society have been forced to think and decide what other possibilities may be available for them, apart from marriage and religious vows. For many women, life has been a journey dedicated to others rather than to oneself. Today, women's situations have evolved considerably, at least in most western cultures. Nowadays, women are able to decide not to be passive and to continue fighting the battles of feminism. Women have had access to more areas that were not available to them before. Women can also decide to have a life of their own and to live to please themselves. These feminist women are discovering themselves. They are dealing with both individual and collective fields. This feminism is searching for a material and conscious equality. According to Natasha Walker, there is also that feminism that looks for the political equality: 'Above all, the new feminism is materialistic. It concentrates on the material reality of inequality' (6).

Roberts, on the other hand, does not concentrate on a material equality but her writing is focused on personal experiences and feelings that aim to be part of the history of women. In this regard, this contemporary writer highlights the importance of telling stories from the inside. From this shared and public awareness these stories can be formed by personal experiences: 'Women have always been aware of the need to use their own experiences as a starting point of feminism' (Walker 56). When dealing with feminism, women's role in the world is considered. Roberts's protagonists participate in this revision of history to tell new stories that deal with the heroines' personal experiences which are publicly shared and criticised.

Storytelling happens on a daily basis at home, at work or at the local shop. Everyone listens and tells stories during their life. Mature mothers and grandmothers embark on the practice of storytelling when they compare divergent situations but parallel experiences. That influence between grandmother, mother and granddaughter can be huge, especially if narratives keep moving from mouth to mouth up to the point of becoming history or myth. This emotional and mindful link among grandmothers, mothers and granddaughters is manifested in Roberts's literary production because the text is shaped after a story is told. Roberts's stories are consequently written in order to be part of a women's writing archive. The creation of Roberts's novels evokes a literary archive formed by women. The proposition of a women's archive will be recurrent in this feminist writer.

In *The Book of Mrs Noah*, for instance, there are some references to the heroine's grandmother. She is the wise woman who gives Mrs Noah inspiration to start writing. The protagonist seeks to find that space or moment in which she can go back to her necessary past: 'If I have my grandmother's blessing I can leave for the Ark without too much fear. I need my ancestor at my back' (14). This particular episode focuses on that search for the heroine's ancestors, especially for her grandmother's nurturing stories. This search will provide the protagonist with inner awareness as she has embarked upon her unconscious. In Mrs Noah's writing process, there are references to memories and death. The latter connects to her ancestors. Mrs Noah has started to remember her past but she is not satisfied with her memories and that is the reason why she aims to come to an end with her insightful recollections in order to reconstruct her story. Mrs Noah's journey through her memory and through acknowledging dead women concludes when she reaches her unconscious, mental space that allows her freedom and comfort to create a text: 'I drop past floor after floor of memory, down past death, down to the bottom floor of the unconscious' (14).

This search for references of an earlier period by means of the figure of the grandmother is also depicted in *The Visitation* (1983), where Helen maintains an intense bond with her grandmother, now transformed into a young and beautiful witch. This women awareness passed from grandmother to granddaughter grows in Helen who becomes a curious character exploring her identity and knowledge as a woman. Helen's grandmother symbolises various stories which evoke other heroines who have not been heard, at least not until this moment. Roberts highlights in this passage not only the story of a woman but the importance of having a women's collective awareness:

> She changes herself into a witch. She is young and beautiful ... The witch is full of mystery, and tremendously old, despite her look of youth. Her wisdom goes back years, beyond the day of Helen's birth, beyond the nine months in the womb, to the generations and the centuries beyond. Her ears can hear the echo of old voices, ancient griefs, and far-off battle cries (101).

Not only women's collective archive is imperative in Roberts's work, but words at the time of rewriting stories of women who aim to find a language that is identified with their bodies. Feminists such as Judith Butler have stressed that the language of the patriarchal society is one and static, and does not allow new meanings that can express the woman's body, which is, on the other hand, many and in constant movement:

> For Feminist theory, the development of a language that fully adequately represents women has seemed necessary to foster the political visibility of women. This has seemed obviously important considering the pervasive cultural condition in which women's lives were either misrepresented or not represented at all. (Butler 1990: 1)

When dealing with women's writing, it is essential to build up a language that expresses women's essences and what they desire instead of what society has predicted for them. This language for and by women bestows the creation of new texts. The word acquires a new sense because women's language has to do with women's body. Michèle Roberts, together with Virginia Woolf, among others, has stressed the imperative significance of the word *woman*. What are its connotations? For Roberts, it is necessary to review and make the meaning of *woman* up in order that its various interpretations can be well thought-out: 'I found the word woman so fascinating. What does this word mean, do I have to accept the definition or can I make up my own definition, 30 years later I'm still writing about woman and finding new meanings' (*BBC*).

Virginia Woolf also argued that the term *woman* cannot be represented by dichotomies such as good or bad, passive or active. For Woolf, *woman* is indefinable and changeable. The Victorian author states that it is difficult to define *woman* when they have so many fields and areas to know and experience by themselves: '[W]hat is a woman? I assure you, I do not know. I do not believe that you know. I do not know that anybody can know until she has expressed herself in all the arts and professions open to human skill' (5). Another remarkable feminist that addresses the significance of the word *woman* is Julia Kristeva. The Bulgarian philosopher draws attention to the impossibility of defining *woman* because the language established in our society is limited. Being a woman means to be away from boundaries and ideologies. Being a woman cannot be registered in fixed principles because the term is constantly being modified: 'In 'woman' I see something that cannot be represented, something that is not said, something above and beyond nomenclatures and ideologies' (137).

The various meanings of the word *woman* are focal points for Roberts. Feminism has been seen as a movement that nurtures women and that allows women some space for constantly fighting back. For Michèle Roberts, feminism is home, a place where she can scrutinise and participate in women's history, language, religion, culture and literature. Roberts's contribution to feminism is expressed in her works of fiction. The feminist writer revises histories of women in order to rewrite them. For Roberts, the difference is that women's stories are not only revised but rewritten with a language that belongs to the body of the woman who is writing. Roberts's heroines are usually the narrators of their own accounts. Roberts's protagonists highlight the importance of combining body and language when writing as women. With this in mind, the following chapter of this book will be dedicated to Roberts's heroines as both individual and common beings.

Michèle Roberts's heroines

When studying novels, one has in mind imaginary characters. The purpose of literature is to make the reader not only picture other worlds but question social, political and historical issues. Michèle Roberts uses historical heroines in order to find inspiration for creating new characters and new stories. She has been inspired by women who belong to different disciplines: religion, society, literature and mythology. Roberts has been inspired by the Virgin Mary, Mary Magdalene, Mrs Noah, Saint Teresa of Ávila, Mary Wollstonecraft, Charlotte Brontë and other women. Roberts provides, however, a new perspective, a new beginning, and another story in which the contemporary reader participates. With Roberts's heroines, readers are invited to question history and its true purpose. In Roberts's novels, the intention is to modify history by questioning the past and by highlighting the creation of stories that are focused on women's inner selves. These different women will stress multiplicity instead of contrary dichotomies. The purpose of Roberts's heroines is to extinguish both the good, passive, beautiful woman, and the bad, active, beautiful or ugly woman. Roberts aims to end with that dichotomy that has separated women. Instead, this feminist writer explores the potential union of opposites in the same woman.

In *Food, Sex & God: On Inspiration and Writing* (1998), Michèle Roberts writes about the importance of including contrary aspects as part of one's identity. According to Roberts, imagination or the inner self we are discovering by means of our own bodies, cannot be restricted to contrary binaries but it should join and celebrate both features in the same identity: 'We won't label it either little angels or little devils, because we know that inside us are both little angels and little devils, both mother and child, both man and woman, both darkness and light, both good and bad' (22).

If the first novels written by Roberts are considered, one can observe how this feminist writer has focused on two marginalised characters for the Catholic Church. On the one hand, the Virgin Mary is the ideal woman, respected by the fathers of the Church as she is mother, wife and virgin. For this heroine, sex is prohibited. She is physically and spiritually pure, as she has not sinned. Mary Magdalene, on the other hand, has been presented as the sinful woman who depends on her own body in order to be alive. These two women represent the dichotomy between angel and monster or between virgin and whore. The Virgin Mary is the depiction of the angel as she symbolises innocence, purity, beauty and passivity. On the other hand, although Mary Magdalene may also be beautiful, she is seen as the monster because she expresses herself sexually. Roberts's Magdalene is also active as she decides when she wants to have sex.

If I look into this dichotomy between the angel and the demon, or between the I and the other in contemporary feminist narrative, I can make reference to other contemporary novelists such as Fay Weldon, for instance, and her popular novel *The Lives and Loves of a She-Devil* (1983). The heroine of this text, Ruth Patchett, will transform her body in order to become that ideal woman that her husband desires, Mary Fisher: 'Mary Fisher is small and pretty and delicately formed' (8). Every one of Weldon's characters is described according to their body shapes. Ruth Patchett positions herself as opposite to Mary Fisher. Mary is admired while Mrs Patchett's husband and society reject Ruth because of her massive body. Mrs Patchett is depicted as the woman who is trapped in her body whereas she is expecting to be accepted by society:

> I am six foot two inches tall, which is fine for a man but not for a woman. I am as dark as Mary Fisher is fair, and have one of those jutting jaws which tall, dark women often have, and eyes sunk rather far back into my face, and a hooked nose. My shoulders are broad and bony and my hips broad and fleshy, and the muscles in my legs are well developed. My arms, I swear, are too short for my body. (11)

The description of Weldon's character is similar to that of a man. Compared to her husband, Ruth is even too tall. There are references to contradictory terms in which the man is positioned on a superior scale than the woman. If a woman is tall, she is not rejected by society if her man is smaller than she is. Ruth's big body is denied. Furthermore, there are references to the hair colour both women have. If the ideal Mary Fisher is blond, Ruth is depicted with brown hair. The former is the lover and the latter is the wife. It has been the society that has created these opposing viewpoints. There is no possibility for the union of contraries in Weldon's narrative but Ruth Patchell does everything that is in her hands to become the admired Mary Fisher, so that she can finally be accepted by her husband and, therefore, by society. Ruth Patchell is not the other but the one and the other. Weldon's heroine was the ugly woman and has now become the beautiful wife who has control over her life: 'A woman's life is what it is, in any corner of the world. And wherever you go it is the same – to those who hath, such as Mary Fisher, shall be given, and to those who hath not, such as myself, even that which they have shall be taken away' (7).[2]

2   Weldon has described in *The Life and Loves of a She-Devil* how women have been separated not only by men but my women themselves. Women have had to fight among each other to get the man's admiration. Maureen Murdock highlights in her article dedicated to the women's journey to encounter their own identity, how the female character is not happy with her self, and as a result, she separates her own persona from her own gender. The following is my translation adapted from the original text which I also present here: 'Our heroine has created an unbalanced situation in her insight that hurt her self ... What she may have lost is a profound relation with her own feminine nature'. '[N]uestra

Going back to Michèle Roberts's work and to the opposed concepts of angel and monster, I would argue that the writing of Roberts's novels deals with this dichotomy but it aims to unify conflicting values. The Anglo-French writer has mentioned how important it was for her to recreate the character of Mary Magdalene as she was allowed to create words that corresponded to her body. For Roberts, the virgin is not only the heroine but also the prostitute. They belong to the same scenario in which they are not longer separated by Christianity but they are happily united: 'Part of the Magdalene's appeal is her challenge to these either/or categories. In the world of the unconscious, virgin and whore dance together, friends. Christianity tried to separate them. Recently, they're getting back together again' (1998: 29).

In *The Wild Girl* (1984), contraries are joined together and it is the marriage of both concepts that shapes the new and real identity of Mary Magdalene. She together with Jesus Christ resurrect from her inner death.[3] When Mary Magdalene encounters Christ sexually, she becomes someone else who is totally free. Although initially man is opposite to woman, this sexual union between Magdalene and Christ breaks those boundaries in order to shape new possible female and male identities, characterised not by their contradictions but by equality. Being equal and respectable to each other is what it is being praised in the following message: '[T]he man and the woman within us has become separated and exiled from each other ... The image of this rebirth is a marriage ... the marriage between the inner woman and the inner man' (110).

This idea of union and of a corresponding matrimony between man and woman makes me have in mind the term *phallocentrism*, already mentioned by feminists such as Hélène Cixous. According to

---

    heroína ha creado un desequilibrio dentro de sí que la ha dejado marcada y herida ... Lo que puede haber perdido es una relación profunda con su propia naturaleza femenina' (19).

3   Resurrection is a Christian doctrine and it will be significant when analysing Roberts's Mary Magdalene but it will be in the chapter dedicated to sex and religion, where further analysis on this topic will be explored.

Cixous, the system imposed by society is based on oppositions, and especially on separated differences between men and women: '[A] two-term system, related to 'the' couple man/woman' (1975: 91). This devalued system has not only been negative for women in history and society, but this classification has conditioned the established relationship between couples to be one. As Cixous suggests, there are more than one possibility for a pair. Couples could be distinctive and perform in diverse ways which allow space for multiplicity. These new options should look into changes and new forms that recreate a new history, free of conditions, a new history that does not have phallocentrism as its enemy: 'Phallocentrism is the enemy of everyone. Men stand to lose by it, differently but as seriously as women. And it is time to transform. To invent the other history' (Cixous 1975: 96).

It is this union of opposites that Roberts highlights in her literary production. If *Fair Exchange* (1999) is analysed, one can observe that different female protagonists contradict each other, exchange characteristics and are finally linked in this work of fiction. *Fair Exchange* is based upon the lives of William Wordsworth, Annette Vallon and Mary Wollstonecraft. Sarah J. Falcus argues that '[t]his novel explores further the marginal perspectives which are ignored in official history as it imagines the experiences of the pregnant, and unmarried, Vallon and Wollstonecraft during the time of the error in France' (171). The beginning of *Fair Exchange* presents Jemima, inspired by Wollstonecraft, and Fanny, inspired by Fanny Blood, as two heroines who are living in a school for women, ruled by the historical Mary Wollstonecraft. Fanny is portrayed as the adolescent who dominates the rhythm and individual pace of other teenagers such as Jemima, who sees Fanny as her example to follow: 'To be singled out by her heroine was so flattering she could not possibly have said no' (18). Jemima is fascinated by Fanny's beautify and feminine qualities while they are both at this boarding school. Jemima shows how big her love for Fanny is: 'Jemima had fallen in love with Fanny because the other girl was everything that she was not. Fanny was pretty, easygoing, careless. She was a favourite with everybody. She was generous with her things ... She was not too clever' (19).

Jemima's words after having met Fanny allow the reader to see the comparative line between both young women, between the *I,* who would be Jemima in this instance, and the other, Fanny. Fanny is what Jemima is not, but what Jemima would like to be. In the beginning, Jemima is in love with that ideal figure accepted by society. In the end, however, Jemima concludes her own exploration by stating that even though Fanny is adored by everyone for her dedicated, female and pleasing activities, she does not want to be dim-witted as Fanny may be. Fanny is adorable but not intelligent: 'The art of femininity in her was like an essence, a perfume she distilled in complete unconscious for the benefit of passers-by' (19). This example makes reference to those characteristics that the patriarchal society invented to separate men and women. Roberts subversively deals with the established separation between women. One is beautiful and feminine, and the other is intelligent.[4] In one of the episodes of *Fair Exchange*, Jemima whispers Fanny the answer to the question about the rivers asked by Miss Everina. After this event Jemima is accepted into Fanny's world because Jemima is the intelligent heroine who is known by her brainy qualities, by her masculine side or by the *animus*, according to Carl Gustav Jung. Fanny, on the other hand, represents the body, the beauty, the feminine side or the *anima* for Jung: 'Jemima instantly bewitched, whispered her names of the rivers, one by one, so discreetly that the impatient teacher did not hear' (16).[5]

---

4   Femininity is a long-discussed term in feminist studies. Simone de Beauvoir deals with femininity in *The Second Sex* as 'that mysterious and threatened reality' that makes a woman (41).

5   Carl Gustav Jung is the psychologist that studied the unconscious psyche. Jung established the differences between *animus* and *anima*. The former is the one which possesses masculine qualities and thus superior values while the latter is classified as inferior and having feminine characteristics (Jung 53). The *animus* takes place in the woman's mind while the *anima* evolves in the man's mind. With regard to women, Jung ends with that dichotomy between good and bad women. For him the *animus* represents the female but with a variety of voices and thoughts. There is not just one reality for the embodiment of women as shown in the following quotation: 'The animus of a woman consists of a great number of preconceived opinions and therefore, it is not represented by a single

After this episode, and once Fanny and Jemima finished their years in Mary Wollstonecraft's boarding school, they had developed a sincere friendship. Once at Fanny's parents, there is an exchange of roles between both friends. Fanny is not the amusing and witty woman anymore. She is more of her time in her bedroom with severe headaches. This reference allows space for *The Mad Woman in the Attic* (1984), written by the feminist critics Sandra Gilbert and Susan Gubar. Fanny is now the passive woman who will get married to William Saygood (inspired by the character of William Wordsworth). That ideal woman constructed by the patriarchal society has accomplished imposed stereotypes as she has even got married, had children and transformed herself into the passive woman who lives isolated in her own room. Jemima, on the other hand, will maintain her independence. Even though she will have a child, a daughter, she will not be compromised on marriage. Jemima becomes a writer instead, pursuing the objectives established by the historical activist Mary Wollstonecraft. Both heroines, Fanny and Jemima, develop active and passive roles at some point in their lives. Roberts highlights the importance of living with opposite values that actually happen in the same character. It is by means of joining opposites, instead of by separating them, that women's identities are being constructed. Jemima and Fanny have been depicted both actively and submissively in *Fair Exchange*. They have been monsters and angels. *In the Red Kitchen* (1990) is another novel that portrays two contradictory heroines. On the one hand, Minny represents the married woman to a rich man, whose life is dedicated to look after others. Minny lacks a place for herself. In this regard, Minny and Fanny in *Fair Exchange* are connected since they are both wives and mothers who are usually isolated in their bedrooms. Because they have been abandoned, they need a place of their own. On the other hand, Flora is the young woman who pays attention to Minny's suggestions to get married.

figure but by a group or a multitude' (my translation). 'El animus de la mujer consiste en un gran número de opiniones preconcebidas y por lo tanto es mucho menos personificable por medio de una figura que, más bien, por medio de un grupo o multitud' (56).

Flora, according to Minny, possesses the sort of features admired by men: youth and beauty. Flora's first thoughts in relation to marriage are negative but with the passing of time, her feelings change as she falls in love with her future husband, George Cotter. This marriage is, nevertheless, presented as a genuine union in which love and equality between the two members are celebrated characteristics. Roberts deals with a positive attitude towards marriage in this particular novel. For this feminist writer, marriage is a happy union between man and woman in which no one is subordinated to the other.

In the eleventh chapter of *Impossible Saints* (1997), there is another reference to contrary terms happening in the same identity but this time, the women who take part in this particular story aim to be equal and as a result become saints. That is the reason why they all have the same hair style and dress up with the same colours in order to put an end to the expression *other*: 'You could no longer distinguish a good woman from a bad one. You could no longer be sure whether the group of women hanging around the butcher's shop ... was a bunch of virtuous wives or a bunch of tarts' (148).

With this body-image renewal, women with short hair and in red dresses have aimed to unify contradictory values in a subversive way. Women of this neighbourhood are not going to have fingers pointed at them for being good or bad, wives or prostitutes any more. They are all the same and therefore they feel liberated. Now, nobody can point at any of them and judge their conditions as virgins, wives or prostitutes because they are all dressed in red, a colour that it is usually associated to women who work in a brothel. These groups of heroines have eliminated that unconstructive image of the woman who uses her body and her sex to deal with prohibited aspects of society. Due to the admired saint Agnes who looks after the beauty of women at a hairdresser's, every woman feels liberated now they are all the same. It is remarkable that Agnes has been transformed into a saint and a heroine for all women in the neighbourhood. Saint Agnes has broken the rules imposed by the patriarchal society by subversively making use of them. There will not be women with long hair and long dresses any longer but the male chauvinist society is being provoked exactly by the signs they have considered negative. The marginalised symbols have now positive connotations in St Agnes's neighbourhood. Red outfits, short hair style for both young and old women imply ending positive and negative separations, and starting a unified liberation of women:

> Girls who looked like Agnes, with cropped heads and skimpy red satin clothes, were not to be seen outside the brothel, or, occasionally, the bar. So the men flocked in to the barber's shop to get a good look at the new hairdresser's help, and business flourished ... The women mopped their red faces, wiped their sweaty hands on their skirts, and drew near to Agnes. They gazed at her enviously. She looked as cool and fresh as well water.
> One by one the women squeezed past Agnes in the shop doorway, sat down in the back room, and had all their hair cut off ....
> The fashion for very short hair swept through the town. Old and young, matrons and virgins, all got rid of their long locks. (147)

Michèle Roberts's protagonists and their relationship with their mothers: the conscious femininity

Michèle Roberts's relationship with her French mother is a distinct aspect of her fictional narrative. Roberts's heroines usually depict this mother-daughter bond either with their own mothers or with maternal figures of their past. In this chapter, I will focus on the relationship between the girl, the mother and the old lady in Roberts's novels, which simultaneously encompass biographical references of this contemporary writer who has confessed how much in conflict her relationship with her mother used to be. Furthermore, birth will be a focal point for Roberts's heroines who, at the same time, are haunted by new beginnings that are linked to the creation of new women identities in the texts. To look into these arguments, I will analyse *A Piece of the Night, The Visitation* and *Flesh and Blood*.

Julie in *A Piece of the Night*, Helen in *The Visitation* and the protagonists of *Flesh and Blood* are telling their stories from a present perspective in order to search for interior consciousness and consequential exterior changes. Past and future references are also bridged in the three narrations. The figure of the mother will be of particular significance for every one of the daughters, whose personalities and identities will be conditioned by their own mothers. According to Shahrukh Husain, mother can be defined as the goddess who raises, reassures and looks after her only child:

> Perhaps the most enduring and widely represented mother goddesses are those, such as Isis or the Virgin Mary, whose mythology emphasizes their relationship with a single child ... the ability of the breast to nourish, comfort and protect is one of the most important and frequently cited attributes of the Goddess. (126)

Furthermore, Clarissa Pinkola Estés argues that there are two different types of mothers: the external mother, who is represented in history, and the internal mother, who refers to the individual and particular mother of every human being. The first mother symbolises the figure of the mother in history and in the social consciousness while the personal mother is unique. She tells her own stories as she becomes a more intimate being: 'Further, this internal mother is made from not only the experience of the personal mother but also other mothering figures in our lives, as well as the images held out as the good mother and the bad mother in the culture at the time of our childhoods' (174).

The connection between maternal figures and daughters is likewise presented in Roberts's work. In *A Piece of the Night*, this feminist writer begins her novel by making reference to the body of the mother together with the action of giving birth. Julie and Claire have been carrying their daughters who are to be now the women who reflect upon feminism and the relationship between women and men. There is a message of continuity through generations with regard to feminism. In *A Piece of the Night* (1978), Roberts depicts the birth of Julie as a rejection. Julie should have been a boy in order that her father would be satisfied and in order that her mother could please her father-in-law: 'Julie Fanchot was born in Normandy, in May, 1949.

She should have been a boy, that was what they wanted, a boy with brown eyes ... a comfort to her father Julien ... a reassurance to her mother Claire that she had pleased her newly-won father-in-law' (2). This particular mother is especially worried about what society has planned for her. She is concerned about what the others may say about her baby girl. Her maternal desire is not to have a healthy baby but a boy that pleases both her husband and her father in law. Julie's mother can be seen as the 'Ambivalent Mother' described by Clarissa Pinkola Estés. According to Pinkola Estés, there are different kinds of mothers throughout a child's life. The ambivalent mother is the one that plays according to society. Her strict role implies to be more distant from her daughter. This mother will aim to shape her daughter in order that she behaves properly as expected by the patriarchal gaze: 'The mother bends to the desires of her village, rather than aligning herself with her child ... A woman in such an environment will often try to mould her daughter so that she acts 'properly' in the outer world' (175).

Julie, the daughter, has been influenced by her mother's attitude towards her life. There has been a long-distance gap between the two women. Nowadays, Julie goes to visit her mother because she is ill. The reader knows, beforehand, that Julie is not praised by her mother as the young daughter follows a lifestyle contrary to what her mother has taught her. Julie reproaches her mother for not having come to visit her. Claire, however, has frequently visited Julie's brother, Claude. Julie shows her personal and most hidden views. She feels rejected by her mother who has never accepted her way of life. Julie does not dedicate her days to live indoors and to look after the house. One of her activities, on the contrary, is to enjoy life and sex, especially if it is with women:

- You've been to see Claude once, Julie reminds her: why not me?
- It's too far, Claire says: too expensive, a trip like that.
- Too dirty, Julie explodes at her: my house is, isn't it? Full of lovely dirty women having a good time, and with a room each all for themselves, and not feeling they have to clean up all the time, and sharing the housework and cooking, and having time to themselves, and a good time in bed. You'd like that

too, wouldn't you? I've got something you haven't got, and you hate it, it really frightens you.
She stops, shaking in terror. Tears pour down Claire's cheeks.
- Go away, Claire whispers: leave me alone.
- It frightens me too, Julie sobs: I'm not used to it, I'm not supposed to have a good time. (90-1)

The Visitation (1983) also begins with a birth. Helen's birth is described in the third person narrator and from the moment Helen is in the womb with her twin brother Felix. In this first page, references to motherhood are brief but significant because Helen's sensations are described at the time in which she is inside her mother. During her time in the womb, Helen is totally linked to her brother. However, the action of giving birth separates brother and sister, man and woman: 'Their mother's body divides them ... She loses him. He is sucked away from her ... Brother, come back, brother ... She has no choice. Where he goes, she must follow' (3). In *The Visitation* Roberts is inspired by the myth of Adam and Eve in which the female figure is being created after the man. Roberts has revisited a religious story in order to rewrite a work of fiction that tries to find its own words. There is another scene in *The Visitation* in which the desire of having a baby, and if possible a boy, is highlighted as a main concern in any family: 'Felix comes out first, the son so much desired, and Helen followed him. Who wants girls?' (109). The fact that mothers prefer to have girls instead of boys is negatively put forward by Michèle Roberts.

Flesh & Blood (1994) is another novel that refers to the figure of the mother from the opening pages. Nonetheless, the protagonist does not choose a birth but she kills her mother instead. It is by the action of killing her mother that the story begins: 'An hour after murdering my mother I was in Soho ... I'd always had a gift for inventing stories ... When I made them up I believed they were true' (1). These lines introduce the heroine's mum in first person narration and it is by means of creation and of making stories up that the account begins. The protagonist kills her consciousness in order to start exploring her own unconscious. She needs to be liberated in order to start creating a story.

That is the reason why the heroine of *Flesh and Blood* has broken any boundaries with her restricted, external and internal mother figures.

Likewise, *The Visitation* brings attention to the relationship between Helen, her mother and her grandmother. The three characters form a constant cycle in relation to their age. According to Shahrukh Husain, the woman's cycle is divided into three phases: the young girl who is not yet fertile; the fertile woman and, ideally, mother of many; and finally, the menopausal and autonomous woman who is now wise and has gained the right to be respected by others (110). With absolute confidence, one can see a parallel between Husain's classification and the female characters of *The Visitation*. Helen represents the young and not yet fertile woman who is still exploring. Her mother is the fertile and mature woman. Her grandmother is therefore the wise woman who is not longer fertile but who represents knowledge and experience.

There is one instance in *The Visitation* in which mother and grandmother are talking about Helen and how grown up she is. Helen is positioned as an object of criticism as the two mature women are addressing Helen's body and her options now that she's becoming a young woman. Helen's body has started to show transformations as Helen is no longer a child but a teenager. Mother and grandmother converse about the possibility of telling Helen about her body changes. Helen's body is just about to be a woman's body. In the following quote, Helen's grandmother is positioned to a more mature attitude as she wants Helen to know about her sexuality and her body as a woman. Helen's mother, on the other hand, is depicted as the protective woman who wants to keep Helen ignorant of her own body. This discussion only keeps Helen petrified as she does not understand what the conversation is about. Helen is portrayed as the woman who is being observed by her predecessors with little opportunity to say what she really thinks. Her opinion as an individual is not well-grounded yet:

> - Has she, you know, begun? Her grandmother whispers to her mother across the cake stand, does she know?
> - No, Catherine Home says, shocked: she's too young.

> \- Well, if you ask me, her grandmother says in her straightforward way: it's time she did.
> Helen stares at the two of them with horror. (9)

In this example, both mother and grandmother debate whether Helen will bear her current body changes. Helen is frightened as she ignores what they aim to tell her. Helen's lack of knowledge is parallel to fear in this argument. Ignorance and innocence are reflected on Helen's face. Helen's mother refuses the option of telling her daughter about the transformations of her body while her grandmother is affirmative. She wants Helen to know about her woman body. While Helen's mother and grandmother continue arguing about the issue of having the period for the first time, Helen starts feeling a ghastly stomach pain and the red stain is visible. Helen's mother is not happy with the physical and moral state Helen is in. Because of her mother's influence, Helen is not receiving the metamorphosis of her body as a celebration but as a depressing experience:

> \- But look at the state you're in, exclaims her mother: red currant stains all down the back of your skirt.
> She seizes her daughter by the arm.
> \- That's not fruit stains. Oh Helen, lowering her voice out of concern for the listening males: what a time to choose to begin. Come back inside and let me clean you up. (24)

These lines also demonstrate that the figure of the mother even complains about the moment in which Helen's body becomes that of a fertile woman. Instead of celebrating this distinct and new act of being a woman, Helen's mother reacts negatively, hiding the event from men. What is Helen's reaction to her body transformations? After having experienced her body negatively, Helen starts feeling guilty and having nightmares. The changeover from childhood to womanhood has negative implications in Helen's mind: 'And that night when Helen awakes crying out from a nightmare of monsters with Aunt Felicity's face her mother does come to sit by her bed and stroke her hair and croon to her: never mind, you'll get used to it' (25). Lack of conversations between mother and daughter increases the monster's consciousness because the protagonist is only scared of everything that is happening to her. Her grandmother, on the other hand, is the woman who nurtures Helen. The wise woman wants to talk to her granddaughter and get her ready to deal with her body and her sexuality.

In *The Visitation* Beth is the character who represents the other side of Helen. Beth could be Helen's imaginary vision depicting Helen's unconscious. Beth could also be seen as a real character, a friend Helen walks with in order to discover her identity. In one episode, Beth is giving Helen some advice about her position in life and her possibilities as a writer. Beth suggests that if Helen is in need of changes, she may ask for them and make them happen instead of remaining in silence, as her mother's attitude may have been. The maternal figure is represented as one that cannot complain, as one who keeps silent instead of asking what she really needs: 'People *should* complain ... All right, don't tell me, I know that mothers can't, that lots of women can't, that the unemployed can't. They are silent, glaring at one another' (87-8).

In *The Visitation*, young and innocent Helen closes her eyes in order to be with her grandmother, that is, with the old and wise woman. *The Visitation* portrays the three states of womanhood. As Marion Woodman suggests, 'While mother and virgin grow together, the old woman is mature in her own self' (133). The old woman or the grandmother is a symbol of experience and knowledge, especially for the young granddaughter who lacks any of those qualities. Mother and daughter, on the other hand, as suggested by Woodman, have a discordant relationship, in which they are both learning from each other. As Woodman continues, '[t]he old woman can be honest; she is not interested in playing games but to go right to the point' (134). The wise woman or Helen's grandmother helps Helen encounter her own identity: 'In her eyes you can see your own self. It is the perfect mirror. You can trust its discipline' (Woodman 134).

In one of the episodes young Helen asks for a meeting with the old woman. In other words, Helen is searching for her inner truth, for her real identity. In order to find her own persona, Helen needs to enter into her past. In Helen's unconscious her grandmother is transformed into a wise witch. Her physical appearance totally changes and the body of the old woman is now shaped into that of a young girl who acknowledges knowledge and experience: 'She changes herself into a witch. She is young and beautiful ... The witch is full of mystery, and *tremendously* old, despite her look of youth. Her wisdom goes back years, beyond the day of Helen's birth ... to the generations and centuries beyond' (101).

This grandmother represents the woman in history. In Helen's unconscious they have a conversation about Helen's identity. The old woman is honest and direct when she speaks to Helen. The wise woman tells the young girl that she must stop hiding herself: 'There's something you're hiding, she remarks in her usual brisk tones: from yourself and me. It's the same thing you hid in that novel of yours ... What is it?' (102). This witch's words liberate Helen who recognises now the reality of her actions and the reason of her limitations. Helen has felt the social pressure as she must be good and write distinctive novels that satisfy her audience. Helen, however, wants to write about sex and not about good and limited actions accepted by society. For that reason, Helen is frightened. She must fight her unconscious which is telling her to follow her inner side, her private feelings: 'I must be top of the class every term, do well, please you. I must write a good novel. Only I am frightened, because what I need to write about will tear the seamless garment of goodness and sexlessness I have worn so long' (102). In the following pages, Helen's reality is dominated by the call she received from her mother telling Helen that her grandmother was not well but unconscious: '[S]he's hardly conscious' (104). Consequently, Helen's grandmother finally dies: 'Winter and darkness win. Nell Home dies, aged ninety-nine, in December, the long night of the year' (105). This death has happened after that meeting between the old lady and the young girl. Helen's grandmother has supported Helen to challenge her fear and, at the same time, to make reference to women in the past. These women have also felt unsure of going after their inner feelings because these emotions and viewpoints could be against society.

Now that Helen's grandmother has died, the questions to be asked are: Who succeeds the old woman now? What role will Helen and her mother Catherine have? Catherine represents now the eldest woman in the house. Catherine is now the wise woman in the family: 'So I, Catherine Home says, her mouth turning down at the corners: am the eldest now. It feels so strange' (106). In the same line, Helen grows the desire of becoming a mother, of becoming a fertile and mature woman. Helen is not completely conscious about it but she really wants to have a daughter, whom she will significantly call Lilith: 'She would like to be pregnant. She hasn't known this. She wants a baby so much. It shocks her. Images of a daughter named Lilith, Lily for short' (110).

Lilith was Adam's first wife. The difference between Eve and Lilith is that the latter was created in equal terms with Adam, allowing her to become more independent than Eve. Lilith's story is associated with the feminist woman because her personality is active, independent and in search for equality. While history has depicted Lilith as a monster who is connected with demons, her image is being used by feminists to recreate her life and her story with positive connotations.

Although *The Visitation* is inspired by the myth of Adam and Eve, Roberts subversively deals with Lilith, Adam's first wife, according to rabbinic and catalyst sources. Lilith has been related to the Jewish folklore. She was replaced by Eve after Lilith had denied acting submissively to Adam's requests: '[S]he demanded to mount Adam during sex and refused to accept that she was his inferior' (102). The difference between Lilith and Eve is that the former was created with the same components as Adam. Adam and Lilith are equal and independent beings. Eve, however, is made of Adam's rib. Eve depends on Adam's rib to be created. Lilith's story has been rescued by various feminist writers because Lilith's personality is characterised by being active and self-determining in search for individual space. Although history has concealed Lilith by presenting her only as a demoniac monster, Lilith's image is being reshaped in *The Visitation* in order that she undergoes a positive and feminist recognition.

The reason why Lilith was replaced by Eve is because Lilith wanted to have an active role and be on top when she and Adam were having sex. Being the inferior being was turned down by Lilith: [S]he demanded to mount Adam during sex and refused to accept that she was his inferior (Shahrukh 2001: 100). It was after this revolutionary moment in which Lilith demanded equality with her partner that Lilith was condemned to abandon the Paradise in order to produce hundreds of demonic monsters everyday (Poorthuis 2003: 61).

Going back to the characters of *The Visitation*, and to the argument of motherhood, Beth, who can be seen as Helen's unconscious, is pregnant. There is a dialogue about being a mother between Helen and Beth. Both characters want to be part of the process of being a mother and that is the reason why they have this conversation on motherhood:

> - Tonight I do, Beth says: tomorrow I probably won't. I go up and down like a seesaw. Can you see me as a mother? I should have thought I'm the type.
> - As much as any woman ever is, Helen replies shortly: there's no such thing as a born mother, you've been telling me that for years. (110)

The following lines of *The Visitation* continue with references to that change of roles between women in Helen's family. Helen is now talking to her mother about how their relationship is today and how it used to be in the past. The distant association between mother and daughter made Helen look for her grandmother. The wise woman gave Helen the love she was lacking from her mother. The young heroine could find in her grandmother a place of safety where she managed to escape from her mother's pressure for behaving properly: '[S]he never allowed her mother to address her with similar words, how she kept her at bay, ran to her grandmother instead, used the old woman as buffer, as refuge' (112). Nevertheless, Helen, transformed now into a mature woman, openly depicts her reconstruction. She thinks of the possibility of having a daughter and how this new being will have to escape from her as well: 'If she ever does have a daughter, just say it's a daughter so that she can use the pronoun she, then she'll have to accept that Lily also will need to run away from home, to hide from her mother, to have her own secret life full of thoughts and especially of doubts' (113). Roberts's highlights the circular course of womanhood. Helen's daughter will have to run away from her mother's limitations in order to become the real woman she is. Helen was a young girl and is now becoming a mature mother and will probably be a wise grandmother.

In *A Piece of the Night,* the relationship between mother and daughter is also addressed. Although the figure of the grandmother is not present, it is relevant to stress that Julie, the protagonist, is daughter and mother at the same time. That means that Julie's mother is also a grandmother. The woman who characterises the old, wise witch is, however, Tante Juliette, who is now dead. In the first pages of the novel, Julie defines what being a mother means. For her, motherhood implies looking after others and forgetting her own self. There are not positive adjectives to describe the figure of the mother. What Julie really wants is to be looked after. She wants to feel like a protected child again. Julie wants to go back to that stage in her life that she remembers with nostalgia because her needs did matter. Helen missed being nurtured by the maternal figure: 'My being a mother cancels out most possibilities of my being taken care of, my needs drown in the claims made on me by other people ... I will go back to Mama and reclaim my place with her, become her child again' (16).

Julie is also concerned about motherhood. After having a child, she does not follow the limitations a mother should have in mind. Claire, Julie's mother and Bertha's grandmother, is an ill lady who is not used to being looked after. Claire has always been concerned with everyone's needs except her own. This situation deals with the mother who offers her entire life to her family: '[S]he must find it hard to accept that she is being cared for. After a lifetime of serving others Claire does not know what to do with rest in her middle-age, she cannot believe that she has needs which other people will offer to fulfil' (24). Claire represents the mother who aims to control her daughter and, at the same time, she is the mother who rejects her daughter's life.

Julie decides to visit her mother. Julie does so because she needs to go back to her past, to her roots. Julie's purpose is to talk to her mother and to feel loved and cared for by her again. The situation is not uncomplicated because as soon as they start a conversation they end up in tears and arguing. Claire only sees traditional ideas about the position of women in society. She does not understand what Julie means by feminism. Julie replies back saying that it is also hard for her because she has to constantly fight back. She not only has to resist the system but also her mother. Julie has not been brought up as a feminist but she has to fight back. Julie is really annoyed because her own mother is not able to comprehend and accept Julie as she is. Both mother and daughter come from the same familiar roots but they are opposed to each other. Both mother and daughter disagree about topics dealing with women's issues because Claire only follows traditional perspectives while Julie is against them and against her own mother as she represents what feminism is not. Roberts highlights that the patriarchal society separates mother and daughter:

> - It frightens me too, Julie sobs: I'm not used to it, I'm not supposed to have a good time.
> - After all I've done for you, Claire weeps into the pillow ....
> - I love you, Julie says with a mighty effort: but I get angry with you as well. Can't you understand that?
> - I never feel angry with you, Claire says ... I just feel so hurt at the things you say. I tried so hard to be a good mother to you. It hasn't been easy. And then you just turn round and say everything I did wrong ....
> - Feminism's about mothers, Julie says despairingly: it's about backing them up
> - You could have fooled me, Claire says ... you hate everything that I believe in. (91)

The link between Julie and old women who belong to the past is remarkable in Roberts's *A Piece of the Night*. On the one hand, Julie addresses her aunt Juliette who gives her mental tranquillity and freedom. Juliette is the old woman that liberates Julie once she is travelling in her unconscious. Juliette helps Julie to recognise her identity and to celebrate her own persona. Juliette allows Julie to know who she is inside as a woman: 'Every Sunday they go on trips together; Tante Juliette is teaching her to fly' (32). This bond between young Julie and her aunt Juliette happens in her dreams. The verb *fly* denotes freedom in the protagonist's mind. The unconscious mental state is represented by darkness when Julie is searching in her mind.

Dreaming and exploring her inner side demands a dark space where the protagonist can find herself and feel liberated. After having learnt how to mentally fly, Julie walks to her auntie to inform her about her decision of flying on her own. Now that Julie has been rescued and nurtured by old women, she needs to continue her journey on her own. It is Julie's grandfather, however, the male figure who wakes her up in order to stop her dream and to make her aware of reality. Julie's grandfather is the representation of the patriarchal society that limits the minds of free women:

> - You stay here, Tante Juliette, she instructs her companion: I want to fly up there on my own. You stay here just in case there's any trouble. If you see me waving my handkerchief, then go for help ....
> - Julie, answer me when I speak to you, will you?
> Her grandfather's voice upsets her concentration. (32-3)

There is another scene in which Julie addresses her husband's great-great aunt whom she admires because this old female character represents the independent woman who lives without a man: 'Julie's husband's great-great-how-very-great aunt is a legend in the family. Travelled alone in south-east Asia she did, alone meaning no man' (110). This old figure is a heroine for Julie, who has been able to chase a different path, contrary to what her mother anticipated for her. Julie's independence as a woman who has achieved everything on her own is written down in this novel.

The relationships Roberts's heroines share with their mothers and grandmothers is a recurrent topic in Roberts's work. This topic is autobiographical as Roberts has always argued how hard it was to fight against her mother's values, and how much love and admiration she felt for her grandmother, who had been the constant muse in her literary production (García-Sánchez 2005). Julie's and Helen's mothers are portrayed in Roberts's works of fiction as women who confine their daughters' options in life. As daughters, they must follow the norms imposed by the patriarchal society. As mothers, they have been trained to act in the same way than their preceding mothers. From generation to generation, daughters have copied the roles of their mothers to adapt their selves to society. Roberts, however, intends to establish the understanding between mother and daughter. Roberts subversively deals with these two women who are linked by familiar bonds and who walk along different paths. *A Piece of the Night* and *The Visitation* have also depicted that connection between the young woman and the mature woman. Roberts has also proposed that other maternal figures such as the grandmother or the great-great aunt may be nearer the heroines of these texts than their own mothers. Even though this feminist writer portrays that separation between mother and daughter, there is also a positive message of encouragement and understanding between both figures.

Sex and religion in Michèle Roberts's novels

Brought up Catholic, Roberts has dealt with the Catholic religion, its limitations and its bad influence on women and their sexuality. Religion has contributed to the separation between men and women in history. It is the Catholic Church which has not only separated men and women but women among themselves with powerful distinctions between good, pure, passive, beautiful, wife and probably, mother (*the virgin*) versus bad, impure, active, beautiful or ugly, maybe mother, but not a wife (*the whore*). These differences between women have been related to their connection with their bodies and sex. In the following quote, Roberts criticises why women have been the responsible beings for human sin. That is the reason why Roberts decided to escape from religion in order to start writing: 'The way that women were treated in the religion I grew up in, which was Catholicism, made me a writer -because women were seen as the source of evil in the world, the source of sin' (*BBC*).

Since the beginning of Christian history, women have been blamed for being wicked. Women's bodies and sexuality were symbols of evil and imperfection. The desires men could have, were generated by women and their bodies. Woman was therefore the blameworthy figure of any repression or desire the man had. As Katharine Moore suggests, sex and sin were synonyms when referring to women. The female body was intended to be a sexual object. Women were considered enemies for the fathers of the Church since Eve's birth. Moore remarks that women were, however, admitted as members of the Church which defended chastity only with regard to women:

> [T]hey reacted fanatically against the increasing immorality of their times. Sex became synonymous with sin and sex was women's fault ... Fear rather than faith took over and in this life-denying atmosphere women were looked upon almost as sex symbols ... Yet, as Christians, the Fathers could not deny that women possessed souls, however mistakenly it seemed to them that God had arranged matters thus, so that though they were looked upon as enemies, highly dangerous from Eve onwards to all men, they were never denied membership of the church ... Chastity for women now became a positive and voluntary virtue. (20)

Michèle Roberts rewrites about this damaged woman in the novel *The Wild Girl* (1984). This fictional text presents the story of the resurrection of Christ in which both Mary Magdalene and the Virgin Mary perform their roles but with changing differences. Christ's mother is not in this novel the opposing woman to Mary Magdalene. While Simon Peter, principal male disciple, disagrees with Mary Magdalene and with women in general, the Virgin Mary advocates belief in Mary Magdalene. Both Marys have a deep understanding of Christ's words and that is what they preach. There is an example in the last lines of the novel in which Magdalene, the Virgin Mary, Salome and Martha have organised a proper home for them to live together and away from their previous place of residence. Magdalene appreciates now that Christ's mother has changed not only her attitude but also her passive behaviour. She is no longer the woman who represented passivity and silence. Now, Christ's mother is able to listen and to communicate anything with absolute freedom. This change of attitude in Christ's mother shocks Mary Magdalene who has to get used to this metamorphosis:

> Mary our mother is still with us ... her tongue has taken on sharpness and a freedom, to which I am still unaccustomed, to say whatever she likes. Before, when I first knew her, her power was expressed more through stillness and listening than through speech. (161)

In the same way, Martha, Magdalene's sister, confesses that she does not want to return to the domestic life now that she has progressed so much. As it happened with the other protagonists, Martha has experienced and developed a metamorphosis in her identity as she only wants to look forward to a changing future, a future the protagonist will have to invent. This character proposes not to follow the rules established by the patriarchal society. Martha searches now to find her own identity. Martha wants to continue exploring her own persona in order to finally encounter the real self that she is. Martha will not look backwards to her previous ways of being an obedient woman. She will not live acting upon commands anymore because Martha can finally go after her instincts: 'First of all, I dislike anyone telling me what I should do. I cannot be obedient simply because it is expected of me. And secondly, I cannot go back to my old way of being a woman. I have come too far. I must find, I must invent, a new way for myself' (135).

When Magdalene confessed that Christ had appeared before her and had left her a message that she must share with the others, Simon Peter was suspicious of her. The message Christ left to Magdalene was about equality between men and women. Simon Peter did not believe Magdalene's word and after a few days, he also confessed that Christ appeared before him to give him another message, contrary to the one Magdalene had already expressed. According to the representtative of the Catholic Church, men are to be leaders. The separation between genders is necessary once again. With this situation, Magdalene asks Simon Peter what the reason for this separation is. Simon Peter replies that Christ was originally a man, not a woman, and due to the danger women can have in the street, especially with regard to sexuality, it is not possible for women to preach God's message as they can be sexually attacked by sinners. Simon Peter keeps on proclaiming that women have another role in the Church, which has nothing to do with that of men:

> - Tell me why I may not be a priest, I cried ....
> - Mary, he said: listen. First of all we knew Jesus as Man. The fact that God became Man ... means that it is for men to come after him and baptise others ... You holy women have a different role. Not a lesser one: a different one ....
> - Amongst disciples, he said: there is no male and no female. In the eyes of God all of us are equal, man and woman, slave and master, as Jesus taught ... But at the same time we live in the world, a wicked and corrupt world where women are at risk of being exploited or abused by sinful men. How can we allow our sister to go about in public and expose themselves to this danger? (131)

The answer provided by the representative of the Church uses the term man as superior and dominating, without having any reflection on the message of equality that Magdalene had previously defended. The man is destined to protect women from evil. This protection implies preventing women from the world of evil but also lack from freedom. Women are not liberated in Peter's world of fear and masculine superiority. The woman is restricted to preach God's message in the church. Women, although equal under God's will, must be protected from evil. For that reason, women cannot be totally active and free at the time of preaching Christ's word in the world.

In Michèle Roberts's novel, Mary Magdalene is a dynamic but rejected being due to religion and society. Magdalene shows her sexual feelings in *The Wild Girl*. The personal becomes public. The personal is about celebrating Magdalene's sexuality, which is no longer negative when referring to a woman. However, in the rewriting of Magdalene's story, the wild girl seems to be awakening as she is discovering both her body and her spirituality. Thanks to the celebration of her sexuality, Magdalene discovers her identity. The wild heroine and Christ have united their bodies and souls. Michèle Roberts is subversively dealing with the position of women in religion, and especially, in the Catholic Church. In the following lines, the protagonist of *The Wild Girl* resurrects from darkness to finally see the light of her identity. Magdalene is at this time able to integrate herself in society, without considering those constrained norms imposed by the Catholic Church:

> Only this time I rose, I pierced through the barrier of shadow and was no longer an I but part of a great whirl of light that throbbed and rang with music – for a moment, till I was pulled back by the sound of my own voice whispering words I did not understand: this is the resurrection and the life. (67)

By reading Magdalene's words, one can appreciate that Magdalene has been reborn. She is now able to listen, but more importantly, to speak with her own voice. She is no longer trapped by the nets of the Catholic Church. Knowing and celebrating her body and her sexuality acknowledges Magdalene's identity.

Correspondingly, Mouse, one of the characters in *The Book of Mrs Noah*, is a woman who shares some characteristics with Roberts's Mary Magdalene. To start with, Mouse's destiny is to become a prostitute. Roberts stresses that some women are given only one chance in life. At the end of the story Mouse is predestined to make love with Turtle, one of the young men who found her in the streets when she was only a baby. In the narrative Turtle brought her up and looked after her until she became a woman. Turtle goes to the brothel without knowing that Mouse could be the woman that he will have sex with. Both will have to act as if they do not know each other. There are cameras controlling the situation. After this first unnatural moment of expression, they meet again on the following morning, but in a place free of cameras. It is in this precise moment when Mouse is reborn after having had sex with Turtle. It is the first time that Mouse feels her own body, her own pleasure. Accordingly, Mouse needs to express herself by means of writing. Mouse's body and language are requited and as a result the protagonist is able to celebrate her own identity:

> They lie on their sides, facing each other ... Pleasure is easy, born of memory, of this comfortable liking, this hunger not held back ... Mouse feels enormous, full, the long valley pulsing while she lies there and laughs, while her knees are liquid and the explosion melts calves and thighs, electric.
> - Let's rewrite the bloody State Dictionary ... let's rewrite every single damned word in it. Let's make our meanings.
> She can talk now. So much to say, to tell. (265-66)

Although Mouse is initially depicted as a destined prostitute, Roberts rescued her to represent the woman who does not follow any imposed norms any more. Instead, Mouse participates in the discovery and celebration of her body, her sexuality and consequently, her identity. Mouse is now awakened. She values her body and sex in a positive way. Both heroines Mouse and Mary Magdalene symbolise new ways of being for women who have been condemned by society or religion. None of these protagonists embodies a passive or negative role when dealing with their sexuality. On the contrary, they enjoy their bodies, their sexuality and their identities. Neither Magdalene nor Mouse will use their bodies to satisfy others (men), but to please their own needs. These heroines are positioned as subjects who are now active with regard to their bodies. The body obeys the needs of its owners. The body is no longer an object for others to consider but a subject that acts according to its demand.

Another novel that deals with body and sexuality is *Impossible Saints*. In this account, different stories about women saints' lives are told. For that reason, it is paramount to examine the term *hagiography*. As Thomas Head conveys, 'Hagiography is quite simply 'writing about the saints'. It is a word relatively modern vintage coined from Greek roots: *hagios*, that is, holy, or by extension, saint, and *graphē*, that is, writing' (xiv). If this definition is taken into account, *Impossible Saints* could be analysed as a hagiographical text in the sense that it is dedicated to the lives of women saints, especially to Josephine's, the central character of this novel inspired by Saint Teresa of Ávila.

The structure of *Impossible Saints* is relevant in this regard as it starts and ends with two episodes dedicated to the Golden Room, a sacred place dedicated to conserve human remains of different women who have been considered saints by the Catholic Church. After the introductory episode, the story of Josephine starts and it is alternated by other women saints' stories. With this work of fiction, Roberts uses storytelling for the purpose of shaping a new history based on biographies and personal experiences by women.

Josephine, the central character of *Impossible Saints*, is inspired by the real woman Saint Teresa of Ávila. According to the Catholic Church, the holy person serves as reference and as example to follow. The main goal of the hagiographical text is to tell the lives of saints but also to teach pilgrims good ways of living. This religious literature is centred on saints and it serves if it is read and venerated by religious followers. In *Impossible Saints*, the good relationship that the child Josephine had with her mother and with her cousin Magdalene is first narrated. Once the protagonist becomes a woman, and after her mother's death, the only option left to her is to be confined to the doors of a convent. Josephine shares with the other women saints of the novel the patriarchal influence they have experienced in relation to their body and their sexuality. I agree with Sonia Villegas López when she suggests that Roberts usually insists on the paternal authority to keep women to enclosed spaces, being either the house or the cloister (4).

All the heroines of *Impossible Saints* have suffered violence and marginalisation by the patriarchal society, represented by either the figure of the father, the brother or the husband. Women used to get married either to God or to a husband. Roberts demonstrates that women used to be separated among themselves by the patriarchal society with the intention of reducing their possibilities to be either wives or nuns or prostitutes. An example is illustrated in *Impossible Saints* with regard to widows. According to this patriarchal hierarchy of women, the widow was considered inferior to other women. This account is depicted in chapter three where the story of Paula is narrated. She is now a young widow who is not allowed to express her sorrow publicly as it is considered a sin. The woman is told to maintain her position and not to express her feelings, neither in relation to pain nor in relation to happiness or pleasure. Paula's father compares her with Julia, her youngest sister, who is the distinguished woman in the family because she preserves her virginity. Indeed, this episode subversively criticises the condition of women in history. It illustrates that the woman and her body are extremely connected to her sexuality. If the woman uses her sexuality voluntarily and consciously, she loses power in the patriarchal world. Women are then seen as human beings who are constrained by the male voice:

> Your sister may be ten years older than you, Jerome said to little Eustochium, but you are her superior. You're a consecrated virgin, and she's just a widow ... As a virgin, you are, technically, superior to your mother as well. Your crown, my dear, will be the brightest. You are the flower of the women in your family. (23)

These words from the authoritative father to the prestigious-virgin daughter neglect the woman who is not sexually pure. Julia is superior to all women as long as she preserves her virginity. This constant rivalry among women has been generated and established by the patriarchal society, which has openly manifested its preferences with regard to accepted or rejected women.

There is a demystifying message of the woman angel and the woman monster, according to Catholic thought. *Impossible Saints* dedicates two other women saints' stories to Thais and Mary of Egypt, who are depicted not only as saints but also as prostitutes. Saint Mary of Egypt is in charge of the priest Zozimus's house in Gloucestershire. The role of Mary is only secondary at the beginning of the story as it is Zozimus who is presented as the main character in the story. When this episode is developed, Mary becomes the protagonist in the story since she has gone to Egypt to turn into a prostitute. Roberts makes the figure of the marginalised prostitute a heroine in this account. Now in Egypt, Zozimus and Mary meet and Mary is the one who invites Zozimus to her house. The male character is amazed by the wealth Mary possesses in her house and Mary tells him that everything she has is thanks to her sex and the celebration of her sexuality, one of the heroine's most celebrated qualities: 'I discovered I had this brilliant talent for sex, Mary began: I really loved it and I was very good at it. Of course, being single, and being Catholic, I tried to damp myself down. But once I'd left Blodwell I said to myself: come on girl, you only live once' (301). The feminist writer is attacking the Catholic Church. *Impossible Saints* allows a diversity of women to become saints. These holy women are saints in the sense that they celebrate not only their minds and spirits but also their bodies. Mary of Egypt, like the other protagonists of *Impossible Saints*, has learnt to discover and love her body and, accordingly, her persona.

This figure of the prostitute, who has been used and attacked by the patriarchal society, is a recurrent topic for feminist writers such as Michèle Roberts. After centuries of physical and sexual oppression for women, Michèle Roberts, together with other feminist writers, participates in the narration of characteristics and events that identify the prostitute in order to sympathise with her: 'Their sense of physical oppression and sexual exploitation led feminists to identify with the prostitute, a figure who had always aroused sympathies, however covert, of women novelists' (Showalter 1977: 193).

Josephine is another heroine that celebrates her body and sexuality in *Impossible Saints*. After her father's death, the protagonist feels empty and goes to live with her cousin Magdalene for a while. During this time, Josephine realises that so far she has lived to satisfy others. The same has happened with her writing. She has been conditioned to write what others expect of her, not what her inner world tells her to write: 'It was just the same with writing, she said: I was always trying to please other people' (137).

It is after her father's death and at Magdalene's house when the priest, Lucian, and the nun, Josephine, start having a romance and thus a sexual relationship. Magdalene's house serves as a place where both characters can liberate their bodies and their minds. Magdalene's house is presented as a residence where different parties are celebrated and where Josephine can forget about her constrained life in the convent for a while. A nun and a priest are sexually and secretly liberated at Magdalene's house. Michèle Roberts depicts, in the following lines, both the masculine and feminine religious figures, being trapped in the restrictions of the Church, which condition their lives and desires. These deprived feelings are manifested in the loving relationship Josephine and Lucian create:

> Or if she has tiptoed downstairs to join Lucian on one of the wide sofas in front of the fireplace, where he slept when he stayed the night, she would share breakfast with him outside in the garden ... Josephine hid her nocturnal expeditions from Isabel. She believed herself to be very discreet. Her niece slept

late in the mornings, and, by the time she struggled bleary-eyed from bed, Lucian was long gone. (178)

This quotation also refers to three main characters in *Impossible Saints*: Josephine, Lucian and Isabel. These parties not only join Lucian's and Josephine's bodies but also Isabel's and Lucian's. Josephine's niece will encounter her first sexual experience by means of Lucian, who is now considered an expert in these love matters. Because Magdalene was having a fancy dress party, Isabel was mistaken for Josephine but she did nothing to stop the misunderstanding. Isabel plays her auntie's sexual role. Isabel's mask and body allow her to have sex with Lucian: 'In a moment of clarity cool and hard and cutting as glass she thought I am Josephine and she held out her hands to her aunt's lover who spun her close to him, clasped her in his arms and expertly swept her about, forwards and back' (215). Isabel consciously pretended to be her auntie to deliberately have this personal and dishonest experience.

In *Daughters of the House* (1992), Michèle Roberts is inspired by another historical personality and second woman Doctor of the Church, after Saint Teresa of Ávila: Saint Thérèse of Liseux. Once again, Michèle Roberts questions Saint Thérèse of the Child Jesus and the Holy Face's interior and exterior life as a woman in the nineteenth century. Roberts points out that the French Carmelite nun is only depicted ideally by the Catholic Church. It is the religious institution which has created this non-real woman. If one reads Saint Thérèse of the Child Jesus's autobiography, she is seen as a human being 'damaged' by religion and society. Roberts underlines that Saint Thérèse of Lisieux is another woman who has written about her feelings; she always felt guilty about her body and her sexuality:

> The ideal Thérèse comes out via the Church, and via a sentimental cult of Victorian piety, and Victorian notions of women, so lovely, sweet and good ... If you read the autobiography, it's very interesting ... it is about anger, loss, terrific suffering, doubt, sex, about her relationship with her father, it's a fascinating document. (Galván 369)

The character of Thérèse is being rewritten in *Daughters of the House*. Roberts's Thérèse is not the perfect heroine that the Church has wanted to depict but she is a real and reflective woman who expresses her feelings and her repression with regard to her body and her sexuality. By reading her autobiography, Thérèse manifests that she is quite a real woman, opposed to the ideal personality everyone knows. For Roberts, the Catholic Church is not good for women as its only purpose is to enclose them in monasteries or houses and control their activities:

> I don't think that Thérèse in *Daughters of the House* is that awful, but she's quite damaged by conventional piety ... She could have been all right, but I think that form of Catholic piety for little girls isn't very good for you, because it does damage you, it makes you feel guilty about your sexuality, it makes you feel guilty about your body. Catholicism is not good for girls and women. (Galván 369)

This culpable feeling has pursued women since the creation of the world. According to Christianity, Eve was responsible for the original sin. In *The Visitation* (1983) Helen is compared to Eve. Helen's relationship with her twin brother Felix is compared to the existing relationship between Adam and Eve in the Garden of Eden. Helen, like Eve, is depicted in a huge garden in which she is looking for the union between both sexes. Man and woman have been separated and negatively opposed to each other since the beginning of humanity. Now everything is different because Helen has found an unconditional union with her brother. This exciting moment takes place when Helen finds a statue of Adam and Eve represented as inseparable beings: 'This is how things should be: the masculine and the feminine so tightly joined that they are inseparable one from another' (170-71).

This agreement between opposites makes reference to Carl Gustav Jung's theory in which animus and anima are states developed in both men and women. Jung has said that men and women have masculine and feminine characteristics in their identities. Roberts has also interpreted these two possibilities in her works of fiction. Accordingly, in this journey through Paradise, Helen finds new references to the bond she maintains with her brother. Incestuous guilty feelings are declared when Helen expresses sexual desires towards her brother: 'Incestuous wishes, for which she was punished with blood' (171). Helen and Eve play similar roles as they both identify with wickedness: 'The mark of the forbidden apple on her hands ... Helen is the evil one' (171).

In *The Visitation* the woman, being Eve, Helen or any common woman, is imagined as a negative and guilty being whose punishment is exposed in her monthly periods and especially, in the painful labours she has been subjected to after having been punished by God: 'And he [God] said to Eve: you shall labour to bring children forth, in pain' (172). Helen experiences a rebirth in the novel as she encounters her identity. With the help of her friend Beth, Helen deals with the problem of being a guilty woman. She is now allowed a new beginning, a new start to write and find her own way. *The Visitation* can be considered the created element that Helen has been able to shape. This writing is what Helen has given birth to with her own words, language and body: 'She (Beth) commands her (Helen) to sing of her redemption, her life, to speak, to write. She orders her: now define self, now define woman. The heart of the labyrinth is not the end, but another beginning. Start to write' (173).

In *Flesh and Blood* (1994), Michèle Roberts tackles women's sexuality by means of the character of Felicité. The protagonist of this fictional account is engaged to Albert but she finds sexual and intellectual liberation with George, the painter. Felicité, as her name indicates, underlines how joyful she has felt after having had sex with George. She now sees that her wedding commitment is not what she really desires as it will bring her sexual freedom to an end: 'I'm not sure really, she said: that I do want to marry Albert, you know. I've been thinking I'd like to be a painter, like you ... You don't understand I want to be free like you' (53). The intellectual and bohemian life this heroine has experienced with George, the artistic figure, makes her aware of the options she could have in her life other than marriage. Roberts, however, portrays the sad side of the story as Felicité receives her bodily punishment from her fiancé. Felicité's passionate moment is transformed into penalty, pain, sadness and loneliness.

Felicité has not followed the norms of the patriarchal society. She has broken off her engagement and she is therefore being stigmatised. The only remaining moments for Felicité are those dedicated to express her inner feelings, her pain and sadness. Through her conscious words, Felicité is able to tell her story, the story of her life and the story of evil which she has suffered in the flesh and in her mind. Writing becomes a healing process for Felicité:

> [T]here was no one to help her. All she had were words, crashing inside her head like waves on the beach, words which filled her and blotted out the pain, lifted her up, high up, till she could see herself lying crying on the bed while Albert rolled over and sat up, words which relentlessly told her a story about evil. (56)

This episode has depicted that Roberts's female heroines have been conditioned by their sexuality and by the Catholic religion. The works of fiction correspond to the history many women have faced not only in the past but even today. Six novels have been presented as examples of fictional texts that have portrayed different heroines, sometimes inspired by historical women, who have suffered the negative consequences of their bodies and sexuality in their identities. Roberts has presented these women as sinners who have been imprisoned in a history mostly written by men. Michèle Roberts has been inspired by female, religious characters such as Mary Magdalene, the Virgin Mary, Saint Teresa of Ávila, Saint Thérèse of Lisieux, Mrs Noah or unnamed women who have also survived their difficulties in life. Even the myth of Adam and Eve has been revisited, especially in *The Visitation* with the purpose of looking into the origin of the world, the origin of the separation between man and woman, the origin of history. Roberts, nevertheless, has intended to offer her heroines language to express themselves and to tell their personal stories from within. These women will be able to find their identities by means of putting down exactly what their bodies feel. Magdalene or the character of Mouse is presented in their accounts as women that after having been rejected by using their bodies and their sexuality are liberated when actively exploring their bodies. This acceptance of the protagonists' bodies has allowed the heroines to find and cherish their own identities.

Roberts's heroines have manifested their physical freedom by means of sexuality and writing. Roberts's protagonists use their own words to criticise religious and historical accounts in which women have not been considered and, if they have, they have only been seen as passive, evil or negative. Michèle Roberts has wanted to reveal the importance of telling personal experiences to make them public and shared. It is in *The Wild Girl* (1984) where the Virgin Mary asks Magdalene to write a book about their stories so that their lives and experiences can be preserved for future generations, and they can preach the real message of equality that Christ has taught them: 'As she says, it was she, acting on the instruction of the Saviour, who commanded me to write it. I am afraid to show it to her ... It is my last gift to her, this writing, and I want her to find it pleasing' (161-62). Magdalene's reaction is that of apprehension because it is a big responsibility to link her body to her language and to write a manuscript. She wants at least Christ's mother to be satisfied when reading her manuscript. This textual creation will have a different impact on traditional readers who are not used to this message of equality. For that reason, the narrator fears the present and future reactions, although Magdalene finally completes her writing in the shape of *The Wild Girl*.

This chapter has also demonstrated that Michèle Roberts deliberately criticises the Catholic Church for having marginalised women. In *Impossible Saints*, we have discovered the sexual liberation that a religious man and woman conveyed when their bodies had finally met. The two characters, nun and priest, were sexually and spiritually united without following the confinement of the Church. Instead, they were openly showing their bodies, their sex and, consequently, their personalities. The following chapter will be devoted to this correspondence between body and sexuality or, in other words, between body and soul, which is another dichotomy defended by the Catholic Church and a recurrent topic in Roberts's work.

Body and language in Michèle Roberts's work

Women have always lived depending on their bodies, which have only been considered objects by the patriarchal society. Even today, many women count on their physical image to feel good and fulfilled. History has depicted them in an idealised position, imposed by the patriarchal society. This search for the perfect woman has led women to forget about who they really are as human beings in order to become objects for some men. The voluptuous woman with prominent curves was the model prototype for men some years ago. Today, however, society has favoured the skinny body that rejects her body and her spirit. This perception of the body I am referring to is that of an object. This body is not a subject that performs actions freely. At the same time, body and food are strongly intertwined when dealing with women. How can a hurting body be spiritual as well? Can the body be separated from the spirit? I would like to answer these questions by looking into this connection between body and spirit. The latter is foremost for the Catholic Church because it values a religious experience as a concealed practice. I aim to demonstrate in this section that Roberts's heroines need to express what their bodies feel by means of their private and single language.

In this regard, Michèle Roberts has always defended the interconnection between content and form in her novels. The language that she writes in her literary texts is related to her body and her unconscious. This common characteristic of Roberts's writing style is strongly linked to Saint Thomas Aquinas and his theory about the human being. Brian Davies's study of Aquinas's thought stresses that the human being's body and soul are only represented by the man as the woman lives conditioned by him. Aquinas saw that both soul and body have the same degree of importance and one cannot survive without the other, as Brian Davies manifests:

> He [Aquinas] agrees that we can speak about people by means of the words 'soul' and 'body'. But he does not think of people as bodies plus souls. He holds

> that we are mental/physical units, where 'mental' and 'physical' are not simply reducible to each other. (Davies 209)

For this religious philosopher, both soul and body are needed to fully construct the human being. The man, however, is the person that Aquinas includes in his arguments without any mention to the woman. Body and soul cannot be separated but united as a whole. Body and soul depend on the mind and the language used to express oneself. As Davies continues:

> For Aquinas my human soul subsists because I have an intellectual life which cannot be reduced to what is simply bodily. It does not subsist as something with its own life apart from me, any more than my left hand does, or my right eye ... Aquinas thinks of the human soul as 'the form of the body' and as something subsisting. (213-15)

This union between body and soul in any human being is also argued in Roberts's literary work. For Aquinas, the woman was reduced and devalued, only existing to accompany the man in the process of procreation. In Michèle Roberts's novels, the idea of body and soul integrated as a whole is stressed with special attention to women. Roberts's protagonists are depicted as heroines who celebrate their bodies and that celebration corresponds to their souls. Novels such as *In the Red Kitchen* or *The Wild Girl* draw attention to the harmony of being a woman with a body and a soul. Roberts's heroines need a language that really expresses their bodies.

In the Red Kitchen (1990) is one of Roberts's works of fiction that best depicts features of the body and spirituality. In the first place, the attitude that the two main protagonists have with regard to their bodies needs to be stressed in this analysis. Minny and Flora are the two women who are going to compare their bodies due to their age differences. Flora, inspired by young nineteenth century medium Florence Cook, is, at the beginning of the narration, the young girl who has connections with other spirits. These spiritual meetings will be reflected in Flora's body and language. Minny, on the other hand, represents the mature woman who has a secondary role in the story. Minny gives Flora suggestions about her future as a young and beautiful woman with all accessible options of getting married. According to Minny, once society recognises and accepts your body, the possibility offered to a woman is marriage. This body of the woman is an object that will fulfil maternal accomplishment as the Catholic Church has instructed. In Roberts's novel, the woman's body is seen as an object for the man who decides which one of the two entities, Minny or Flora, is admired by the male society. Despite Minny's suggestions, Flora rejects Minny's piece of advice by affirming that she will never get married, something that she will not maintain as we observe in the conclusion of the story: 'You ought to get married, Flora dear, she prattles on: someone as pretty as you should have no trouble. You won't be left single for very long. I feel sure! All the gentlemen admire you so!' (76).

In the last lines of this novel, Flora declares that her body, portrayed as an object, has been dedicated to obeying what the patriarchal society has ordered. Although she has been silent, Flora understands the commands she constantly receives. Flora knows what to do with her body. She follows Dr Charcot's imperative instructions in order to move her body as she should:

> It is the same thing that Dr Charcot knows how to do to his patients, a message passed in silence through flesh, from William to me; an instruction. It is the same thing I learned with Rosina, with Mr Potson, with Minny: how to receive the thought of the other, from hand to hand, wishes and commands translated, the morse code of the body. (125)

'The London Girl' is another protagonist in *In the Red Kitchen* that directly expresses her dilemma with her body in relation to food. In one episode, this woman mentions how important it is to relish food. After some healing time for having lost her baby, the London woman, who is not presented with a proper name, is now able to savour whatever she eats: 'For the first time in a month I could taste what I ate' (90). For this woman, the body is enemy of the soul, as it is not that pure. The body symbolises sin, according to what the Catholic Church has taught her. One can observe that the London woman feels trapped in her own body. Even though her body was governed and negated by nuns in order to maintain its purification, she highlights that she has used her own body as a way of living. The London girl hates her body because she has the conscious influence of the Church in mind:

> But here I was, stuck on earth meanwhile, stuck with a body. Loathing mine for what was imprinted on it, I was grateful for the nuns' lessons in self-denial, mortification of the senses. But these didn't work: my body alien guest, invaded my pure spirit, dragged my soul back down from where it floated, transcendent. (86)

Although *In the Red Kitchen* identifies the connection of different women at different historical times, Flora and Minny are the two heroines who maintain a direct and physical contact in the novel. This women's narrative is set in the Victorian period in which Flora and Minny live. The London woman and Hattie are only linked spiritually. Of the three stories, Flora is the character who connects with the past by means of Hattie, the daughter of the pharaoh. Similarly, Flora is the medium who spiritually connects with the future by means of the London woman. There is no bodily contact in these spiritual relationships. It is, however, by means of spiritual sessions that Flora has with Hattie that we get to know the pharaoh's daughter's past and the London woman's future perspectives in life.

Even though body and spirit are logically related, the Church has claimed its separation. Saint Thomas Aquinas, influenced by Plato and Aristotle, was the first writer in connecting women to the body, to nature and to the world. Aquinas also saw women as responsible for the world of evil. Women were seen, on the other hand, as the necessary companions of the man in order that they can reproduce new human beings: 'Should woman have been created in the beginning? Yes, replies Aquinas. But only to help man in the work of procreation. Women, he suggests are naturally defective' (Davies 18). If the woman was linked to her body, the man was connected to spirituality, reason and mind. Body, spirituality and mind were separated in the same way than the woman was from the man. Davies stresses that Aquinas fails to recognise women when he continues saying that they depend on rational and strong men: 'They are "by nature subordinate to man, because the power of rational discernment is by nature stronger in man'". Women 'seldom keep a firm grip on things ... since "they are not tough enough to withstand their longings'" (Davies 18).

If *In the Red Kitchen* is reconsidered, Roberts addresses the spiritual side of the woman yet connected to her body. Flora maintains spiritual sessions with other worlds and other beings. Flora's mind is connected to other women of the past and future. She is acknowledged for her spiritual activities. In the following lines, Flora stresses that being part of those spiritual experiences makes her exchange her own being with those of the spirits she encounters, and vice versa. Flora perceives a transformation in her persona, but because she is only seen as an object to connect with spirits, nobody has noticed that change. The only important thing is the result of her spiritual sessions: 'The spirits increasingly give to me of themselves as I leave more and more of myself on the other side. A transfusion. I am increasingly a changeling. I am not the Flora I was a year ago. But who knows that, apart from myself?' (92).

In *Impossible Saints* (1997), there are various references to the body as a religious cult in which different body parts are considered relics. The first episode that introduces the narrative takes place in 'the golden house', a place where bones of women considered saints by the Church are kept: 'The golden house was where the bones were kept ... Thinking to go outside, you went in, to that disorderly house full of dead women' (1). The story of *Impossible Saints* is introduced by Isabel, Josephine's niece, one of the saints and main protagonists in the novel. Josephine, as stated before, is inspired by Saint Teresa of Ávila. Josephine's bodily parts are kept in the golden house chapel. This reference to body parts of dead women who used to live a religious life contributes to imagine and recreate their public lives in women's history. Present women go back to past women to revisit and understand women's history. Isabel retells her aunt's story to her granddaughter. Past, present and future generations are intertwined in this account to value women's history and the importance of storytelling with regard to accounts by women.

Later on in the novel, Isabel tells us about a time in which she used to live with Josephine in the convent. From a present perspective but with constant flashbacks, Isabel tells what a saint like her auntie Josephine really is. The reader gets to know the actual Josephine not only as a saint but especially as a woman. Josephine cannot do whatever she pleases but she will be required to devote her life to religion and to the adoration of God. Josephine is, however, presented as the woman who does everything she wants to although nobody has ever been suspicious of her. Being a nun is depicted as a social role that allowed the heroine to escape from society: 'She appeared tolerant and generous but she was selfish. She did what she wanted. She did her writing and spent hours in bed with Lucian behind locked doors, making love and laughing, I heard them, or she sat about gossiping and trying on her clothes' (273).

As this quotation illustrates, Roberts's heroine does not follow the mandatory principles applied to a religious woman or a saint. Josephine is able to write and to celebrate her body and her sexuality. Josephine gets dressed in other clothes that are not religious. Josephine's body is also naked and sexually liberated. Her body expresses her freedom as a woman who can leave the convent and its limitations. Could the description of this heroine be considered that of a saint? This is the argument that her niece questions in the novel. Isabel's aunt writes books for the Fathers of the Church and therefore, she is restricted to follow some norms. It is demonstrated that Josephine gives her life to the religious monasteries but it is also true that Josephine is presented as the woman who is able to exile and express herself and her body, especially when she is at her cousin's house. This duality between the two lives of Josephine is argued, questioned and distinguished by Isabel. Josephine has secretly broken her vows because she is both a constraint nun and a liberated woman.

The convent has been for many female characters the second way out, after marriage. Women could be handed to marriage from father to husband or to God by enclosing their lives in a convent. The answer to Isabel's question about what saints are shows not only what but how a saint is constructed. As Isabel continues, a saint is what

Josephine is not. Niece and auntie are being compared here. The personal story becomes shared and public: 'Now they are calling her a saint: Could a saint be Josephine?' (273). A saint is also absence. A saint implies that the body is not in the earth any more, but in the dead world. A saint is also invisible because her life in the world has come to an end. All in all, Isabel concludes with the idea that not only Josephine must be considered a saint but her mother, and Isabel's mother, and many other mothers who are now dead and, consequently, saints. Now that these dead women have reached death, they have become spiritual beings who live further away where the body cannot see. Roberts stresses the message in which Josephine's individual life can be compared to that of any common woman:

> A saint is: what I am not. A saint is: over there. Not here. A saint is invisible, I can't see her, she has run away out of my sight, she hovers just ahead of me, the air trembles with her departure, she has gone off and left me, she is the woman I want and whom I can't reach and can't find. She is a woman who is dead. A saint is absence. Always somewhere else, not here.
> Josephine's mother was a saint and so was mine and both are dead. (273)

Josephine's definition of a saint offers some thoughts of liberation for women. Everybody can do whatever they want to by making use of their own possibilities. Josephine is an example of this open-minded woman that does both what she wants and what she is supposed to do. Josephine's mother, however, only did what she was told to do. Roberts maintains a balance between both options. Roberts's saints have achieved possibilities of being saints at least in her novel. This feminist writer is subversively dealing with the strict conditions imposed by the Catholic Church with regard to women. Furthermore, this variety of options makes reference to multiple women who can come from a variety of circumstances and conditions but they are all equally considered independent beings, and why not, saints.

In an interview with Michèle Roberts (published in 2005), there were some references to Mother Teresa of Calcutta and her potential to become the next woman saint for the Catholic Church. This documentary presented by Channel 4 in October 2003 was entitled:

'Mother Teresa, a Saint Making Business' and Roberts openly said that Mother Teresa of Calcutta was 'completely selfless and completely giving herself to take care of others'. Roberts highlighted that Mother Teresa is the ideal woman for the Pope because she is only focused on looking after others. Mother Teresa is the woman who offered her life to others without considering her own needs. Roberts concluded her argument by stating that the Catholic Church has not made any progress with regard to women. According to the Church, the female figure is the passive human being only dedicated to look after others.

With this saint context in mind, it is remarkable to consider that the distinction between spirit and body has separated the latter from its physical desires. According to the Catholic Church, the body should be repressed because feelings and desires should not be revealed. In order for someone to feel spiritually liberated, (s)he must abstain from showing what his/her sexuality has dictated, following the strict parameters of the Catholic Church. Sexuality has traditionally been linked to negative perceptions. For that reason, the body corresponds to reclusive feelings that have been concealed. If the body is repressed, the Church has to find a way out to celebrate that repression. Spirituality, as a result, overcomes sexuality and it is triumphant over it for Catholicism. María del Mar Pérez Gil also addresses that the Catholic Church has separated body and spirit due to the connection between body and sexuality: 'Ludwig Feuerbach pointed out in an essay published in 1851, 'Lectures on the Essence of Religion', that Christians negated the body, the earth and the sexuality in order to transcend them and aim immortality' (154).

This dichotomy between body and sexuality is also appreciated in *The Wild Girl* (1984). The protagonist, Mary Magdalene, is cheerful once she has sexually encountered Christ. Katharine Moore has done a study about the connection between women and Christianity. As she clarifies, women at Magdalene's historical time were almost considered slaves: 'At the time of the birth of Christ, the state of women throughout the civilised world was little better than slavery' (11). If *The Wild Girl* is analysed, one can observe that Mary

Magdalene escapes from her town once her mother has died. She moves to Jerusalem where some merchants rape her on the first night of her journey. Roberts subversively states that this situation was logically expected. A woman who travels alone is considered undomesticated and thus object and body for men: 'There was only one sort of woman, they told me, who roamed about boldly and alone: I understood them to mean wild beast, in need of taming' (15). After having been sexually abused, Magdalene feels, on the other hand, liberated as she will not be accepted for marriage. Her impure body neglects any opportunity of getting married: 'I was brutalized but I was freed; none of the honourable men at home would ever take me to wife now' (15).

Although Mary Magdalene has always observed that she was never valued as a woman, the heroine expresses that since she was a child, she always felt that she possessed a soul. Feeling her soul gave her hope for the life she would have, once she left this world: 'When I was a child I knew, before anyone told me, that I had a soul' (12). Alone, all by herself, Mary Magdalene does discover at an early age the importance of possessing a soul or a spirit that corresponds to her body. Faith, however, is something imposed and instructed by the patriarchal society: 'I learned about our faith through the words of men' (12).

Once Magdalene returns to her place of origin, Bethany, she meets Jesus Christ. It is only during this time that Magdalene feels liberated of restrictions from the very first time. Considered one of the foremost Christ's followers, Magdalene walks long distances on foot. That physical tiredness liberates her body and allows her soul a place in the world. Magdalene's body and soul have been restored thanks to her meeting with Christ. Magdalene has finally found a moment of peace, tranquillity and freedom because she has rediscovered that she possesses a soul:

> I can't express how happy I was. For the first time in my life I felt free ... Walking, I learned, is a kind of prayer, the body swinging along at a steady rhythm as the legs and feet dance ever onwards and the soul is released by the regular motion into the infinite, towards God. I began to acquire peace in my heart. It is a healing thing, I discovered, to walk for hours every day. (57)

This path that Magdalene walks with Jesus Christ is parallel to the path she has to follow in order to find her own identity: 'I began to believe that I travelled towards God, and that I had a soul again' (57). In Roberts's novel, Christ praises Mary Magdalene. Christ presents her as an example of human being. For Christ, Magdalene is the exemplary being that combines body and language by celebrating her sexuality and her speeches. In one of the passages, Christ is situated next to the heroine. Both characters serve as two people that are united in body and soul. The result of this union makes them be virgins again without any names or expressions that delimit them according to sexuality or gender. Christ and Magdalene's agreement embodies a new beginning. Christ and Magdalene's union becomes pure and complete: 'There are those like Mary and me who marry each other in the body and then find the marriage happening in our souls. What matters is that marriage in the soul. And all of us are becoming virgin again, for all of all are becoming a whole' (63).

These positive experiences between a man and a woman are being remembered and told by Mary Magdalene in *The Wild Girl*. Magdalene and her stories have failed to been recognised by the Catholic Church. Katharine Moore, however, suggests that the attitude Christ always had towards women was totally ground-breaking and original. One of Christ's roles was actually to change the conditions of women during such a judicious time: 'His treatment of and whole attitude towards women was so immensely creative, revolutionary and dynamic, that although the Church, following a long way after in this respect, comprehended him not, neither did it wholly deny him' (13). Moore also points out that Christ was a great defender of Mary Magdalene's position in society and religion, which caused a disappointing surprise for the Fathers of the Church, as Roberts has also maintained in her novel: 'Jesus's defence of Mary Magdalene must have astonished as well as appalled the men who heard it ... They come to realise that Jesus thought them to be of equal importance as men in the eyes of the Father' (13).

In *The Wild Girl* all these concealed positions of the historical and cultural Church are portrayed and condemned by Roberts. Jesus is presented as the man who fights to shield Magdalene. Jesus uses Magdalene as an example of human being to be followed. Magdalene's actions in search for equality between men and women are praised by Christ, and as such they are manifested in the religious community. Simon Peter, Christ's principal disciple according to the Church, does not agree with the steps followed by Christ and asks him why he adores Mary Magdalene, a woman rejected by society and religion. Jesus answers Peter by making reference to pure love. Roberts's wild girl loves Christ in body and soul while men are not used to loving in this natural way. Jesus wants to find a change between men's and women's manners. For that reason, Christ suggests Simon Peter to kiss more often, action that emphasises the celebration and liberation of the body. There are not taboo body actions to be hidden anymore. Christ continues with his argument of liberation suggesting that everyone is free to do whatever they want. They can even become God, Christ or Mary Magdalene. Christ positions the figure of Magdalene on the same scale than God and himself. Therefore, Christ offers his followers the potential of being whoever they want to be. In Roberts's novel, Mary Magdalene has been made equal to Christ. Peter does not accept Christ's message and asks him to exile Magdalene from the group. In the following lines, Roberts have maintained the male-chauvinist position of the time. Despite Christ's message of equality between men and women, women's rights to live as human beings were rejected as they were merely seen as slaves. Women were totally inferior to men:

> - Why do you love her more than any of us? Simon Peter burst out ....
> - Why not ask why I don't love you in the same way as I love her? He replied ....
> Mary loves me completely, Jesus answered him: body and soul. Our kisses demonstrate that we are lovers of each other and lovers of God, nourishing each other, conceiving and giving birth between us to God ....
> [M]y disciples, are different. You can see the Spirit and become Spirit. You can see me, the Christ, and become Christ. You can see God, and become God. You can see the Light, and become the Light. And so, Simon, you can see Mary filled with God, and become Mary.
> Simon pulled away, obviously offended.
> - Tell Mary to leave us, he cried: for women are not worthy of life. (58-9)

Christ defends women and their bodies once again. According to Jesus's words, the male figure has disregarded the woman's body. The woman has been forced to be trapped in her own body without considering her inner feelings. The woman's body is been considered an object that the masculine society must admire, accept, judge or reject. In the following quote, Jesus makes reference to the importance given to the mirror when one refers to women. As he proceeds, women have been slaves of their images because they have to satisfy the masculine gaze. Christ explains that the male society needs to be aware of this condition of the dependent mirror: 'A woman looks in her mirror, does she not, to confirm herself that her face is clean, and pleasing, perhaps even beautiful. Why does she do this?' (73). In the novel, Magdalene answers Christ's question. Roberts stresses this active and equal dialogical participation between Christ and Magdalene. They both converse in equal manners. Magdalene's answer argues that the man has been the responsible being who has only looked for a body in his partner. The man has not been able to look beyond and to appreciate that the woman also possesses a soul. In Magdalene's words, these constant concerns women have had for their beauty have been imposed by the patriarchal mind, and therefore, have enslaved women's appearance: 'Because men have forced her to do it ... foolish men, who only prize a woman for her beauty, and do not see her soul' (73). Jesus supports Magdalene's message by making reference to prostitutes, who, on most occasions, have been forced to sell their bodies and, thus, to lose their soul: 'The body is the mirror of the soul, Jesus answered me: and a man who abuses women's bodies also abuses their souls. That is the way of men who use prostitutes. So much is true' (73).

Women's representation of an identity has been dominated by their bodies throughout history, especially if the actions of the Catholic Church are considered. The Fathers of the Church were responsible for separating the body from the soul. Religion has underlined the division between body and soul, being the latter positive and highly praised, and the former negative and repressed. Michèle Roberts has revisited stories already told in order to rewrite new interpretations of values and positions with regard to women's subjective body in society and religion. *The Wild Girl* is one example of Roberts's revision and reinterpretation of history. The union of contraries is underscored by this feminist author who portrays binaries in her heroines, as it has been described before. The personality of Roberts's heroines is usually shaped by combining dichotomies that can create and celebrate both sides of the woman: body and soul.

Aquinas's claim about body and soul in a man can be complemented if the woman is also included in his analysis. Aquinas's idea would have been accepted by contemporary feminists such as Michèle Roberts if he had not excluded women from his criteria. The woman is not only body but mind. If history had considered women part of this process of evolution, today we would not have been writing about these political, social and discriminatory gender issues that have only undermined the position and consideration of women in history. Nevertheless, I like to think in the conscious awareness many women and men maintain nowadays with regard to women's situation in the world:

> Aquinas's teaching on the nature of the human person is close to that of Aristotle's *De anima*. Aristotle thought that people are not two things, mind and body, but complex unities both mental and physical ... He agrees that we can speak about people by means of the words "soul" and "body". But he does not think of people as bodies plus souls. He holds that we are mental/physical units, where "mental" and "physical" are not simply reducible to each other. (Davies 209)

PART B

Michèle Roberts, the memoirist

This second main section is devoted to *Paper Houses: A Memoir of the '70s and Beyond* (2007). As this text takes the form of an autobiography, happening in a particular period of time, I would like to deal with personal and public spheres at the time of writing as a woman. *Paper Houses*, mainly set in London, will also take the form of a work of fiction. This time, however, past and present, true and false accounts participate in the reader's perception to tell the story of a woman who is constantly moving places. This woman-writer and protagonist, Michèle Roberts, aims to find a home and, therefore, her identity as a woman and as a professional writer.

As Michèle Roberts pointed out in the introduction of *Paper Houses*, 'I am a witness, and I am an actor too. Writing this memoir joins up all the scattered bits of me, makes them continuous, gives me a conscious self existing in history' (6). Roberts's conscious past becomes constructive and active in this autobiographical work. Her memoir activates the writing process with memory backing it up. The memoirist uses language, autobiography, story-telling, history and fiction to create words that give form to her text. There is a connection between Roberts's past narratives in the form of diaries, and her new readings of them. The feminist writer rereads her diaries and invents a new identity that it is portrayed in her memoirs from a present perspective: 'Who was that 'I', that young woman of twenty-one? I reconstruct her. I invent a new 'me' composed of the girl I was according to my diaries, my memories (and the gaps between them), and the self remembering her' (14). Nicola King suggests in *Memory, Narrative, Identity: Remembering the Self*, that when one is in the process of writing an autobiography, "[i]dentities are not discovered, but rather actively constructed by individuals': reading and writing are constitutive of this process, which also always takes place within a particular social formation' (King 7). Roberts's social, political, educational, family and friendly environment did form part of her identity then and of what she has become today. There is a process of change and continuity but also, of rescuing her past and putting it on paper.

In *Paper Houses*, Roberts becomes the central character of her story. The first person narrative, which is part of the autobiographical language, makes the story more truthful and reliable. Roberts admits that she 'learned how to tell stories first of all through writing fiction' (6) and it is by means of this unreal story telling form and by using the first person narrator's voice that the protagonist opens some episodes of her life to contemporary readers. Likewise, Roberts intertwines her personal story and description with the political, social and historical moments of the 1970s and 1980s, mainly in London. In this regard, we see both Roberts as the observer and as the young woman who is being observed. With her memory, Roberts is able to recreate notions of self-identity 'in a narrative which attempts to recover the self who existed 'before'' (King 1). Roberts uses the 'She' subject as a reader of her previous diaries and, equally, the *I* voice tells her own story. Roberts is a protagonist, researcher and writer of her own diaries and of her own memoir. There is a split of both identities which are unified at the end of the self-discovery narration. Roberts was that girl in the 1970s and 1980s. This feminist writer keeps an essence of her past that is projected into her present writing moments. As the writer continues: 'She's [the girl who wrote her diaries] a character in my story and she tells too. She's like a daughter. Looking back at her, thinking about her, I mother myself. I listen hard to her silences, the gaps between the words' (14). *Paper Houses* is a journey around places. *Paper Houses* is also a rootless performance of the relationship between communal compositions and the creation of the individual consciousness that Roberts creates. This memoir is a text 'of the construction and deconstruction of the myths of the self' (King 35).

Paper Houses: A Memoir of the '70s and Beyond is about love, identity, sex language, body, and above all, about creating, inventing meaning, and becoming a woman and writer with Roberts's own language and space. *Paper Houses* is a metaphor of a place in which Roberts finally finds a place of her own and a place where she can take on her personal meaning. *Paper Houses* is about Roberts's body and language. The protagonist-writer is homeless and searching for knowledge and adventures that construct her identity. Language, experience and walking around London gave Roberts inspiration to create her paper house in order to become the prolific writer that Roberts is today. In this second part, I will devote my analysis to four chapters dealing with the female *flâneur* experience in London. I will also look into Roberts's memoir by analysing the personal and public spheres of the writer-protagonist and the historical movement she lived in. Then, I will analyse the structure of the memoir itself and its correspondence to modern and postmodern techniques. Finally, I will dedicate an episode to the correspondence between history and culture in *Paper Houses*. I will look into the historical time of the 1970s and 1980s in such a city, London. This last argument intertwines with the first chapter of part B in which there are constant references to the female *flâneur* who strolls and travels around and in London. These journeys will be necessary for Roberts, the memoirist and the novelist.

Michèle Roberts's memoir: walking as a woman *flâneur*

> These were two of the adventures of my professional life. The first – killing the Angel in the House – I think I solved. She died. But the second, telling the truth about my own experiences as a body, I do not think I solved.
> (Woolf, 'Professions for Women,' *The Collected Essays*)

> I had to go away from that world of categories, into the freer space of poetry and art, with their capacity for subversion of established categories in order to discover my own language and vision, try to integrate body, mind, creativity. Abstract words separated things; I wanted to make art that recombined them.
> (Roberts, *Paper Houses: A Memoir of the '70s and Beyond*)

I have chosen Virginia Woolf's and Michèle Roberts's words to start this chapter because both creative and critical writers are dealing with language and body when writing as women. Both feminist authors are claiming the importance of telling their stories and of putting their experiences down on paper. Both writers of different historical epochs are also dealing with the importance of writing their histories as in the form of a memoir. Roberts's memoir corresponds with the writing of novels. I shall observe that Roberts's autobiographical text shares common characteristics with that of the feminist novel. Equally, the inclusion of the modern female *flâneur* who is travelling and strolling about inner and outer spaces will also be a focal point in this chapter, as it is thanks to observing and being observed that the identity of the heroine of this memoir is constructed.

In *Paper Houses: A Memoir of the '70s and Beyond*, Roberts wanders about different locations in London as a *flâneur/flâneuse* that is first, strolling and second, observing the places she has gone to in order to put her visions down on paper. The feminist writer has used the original term in its masculine form but with the intention of adding the female subject *she*. Roberts is both a modern woman *flâneur* but, at the same time, she is a postmodern *flâneuse* who is exploring with language and content. *Paper Houses* deals with Roberts as both observer and observed. It has a double dialogical purpose of writing and reconstruction. London is the city that Roberts revisits and rediscovers in her diary, her memories and in her experiences in order to present it as the background of her autobiography. The writer becomes the reader and the protagonist of her own text.

Deborah L. Parsons has proposed that women have had different experiences to those of men in the modern city. Even though Walter Benjamin's modernist term *flâneur,* in Parsons's words, is 'both historical figure and critical metaphor in literary and cultural criticism' (2), the female *flâneuse* is inspired by postmodernist context allowing various possibilities to put the woman's experience down on paper. It is impossible to think about the opportunity of having performed as *flâneuse* at the time *flâneur* was coined because women were not able to walk and explore the city alone in the nineteenth century (Whitworth 205).

Michèle Roberts, nonetheless, has maintained the original term, the original language in its masculine form to transform it in a subversive way. The meaning of *flâneur* has been changed to become a twentieth century woman stroller, who walks the streets alone with some kind of freedom. That is the reason why Roberts uses *flâneur* as the original male-context expression but with the female subject *she*. Roberts wants to make reference to the nineteenth century situation of women in city streets.

In the following passage, Roberts highlights and criticises some men's assumptions she had to face while being alone in the streets of London. The nineteenth century mentality used to be to protect women from the streets and to frighten women of the outer world. Contemporary way of thinking allows, however, more freedom and women are commonly seen in public places. In the case of Roberts's present conscious voice, she criticises the patriarchal mentality which can only see a singular type of women who are alone in the streets. Some men's minds still need to be changed. According to the lines below, Roberts felt the patriarchal approach as if she were in need of men. Because Roberts's protagonist was alone in the streets, she was considered a prostitute, someone who could offer sex. Instead of being observed, the heroine wanted to become the 'observer; the one who gazed', the female *flâneuse* (Roberts 2007: 28). Roberts walks the streets to become active and watch that, in fact, it was men who were desperate for sex:

> If you walked around London alone, as I did all the time, presumably looking rather naïve and wide-eyed at the splendour of it all, men accosted you frequently. They assumed you were lonely, all by yourself, and in need of their company. They were certainly in need of sex. (27)

Although London is the urban setting that gives environment to Roberts's account, the protagonist declares that this sexual harassment took place on repeated occasions, while she was also living in Oxford. As readers, we participate in this common situation when a woman is referred to. If we are women readers, we certainly empathise with what Roberts is talking about. Who has not experienced or heard about the frustration of being watched by a man who may ask you something, usually sex, for the simple fact of being alone in the streets, in a café, on a beach, on a park bench or in a bar, for instance? Only if Roberts (and women, in general) becomes invisible, will she then be able to observe freely the city she is walking about.

Oxford compared to London is, nevertheless, described in *Paper Houses* more as a rural area which is more solitary and thus an unsafe place for a woman to be on her own. As it is expressed in the following lines, Roberts challenged society, challenged some men's mentalities in order that she could enjoy the gained freedom of the twentieth century woman:

> The same thing used to happen all the time in Oxford. I had liked to wander alone in the nearby countryside, to sit alone in the meadows reading. Not for long. Men would dart out from clumps of trees, from behind bushes, and start bothering me. I gave up, with inner rage, walking alone in the countryside, but I did not give up walking alone in the city. I refused. (28)

Loneliness remains a necessary condition in the protagonist's mind, not only when she is indoors but also outdoors. There is another example of comparison between London and Oxford when Roberts becomes a Library Scholar in London. Oxford libraries are 'fine libraries'. Oxford libraries cannot be compared to the Reading Room at the British Museum as London libraries imply to enter another world, the world of books. The London Library is described as '[m]ore urban. More worldly. Certainly more democratic' (21). As she continues, the English capital provides everyone with the opportunity to have access to its libraries and its books. Roberts also refers to Karl Marx as an example of a person who applied for a reader's ticket in the London Library (21). Once again, private and public histories are portrayed in Roberts's memoir. Past and present are in a dialogue of constant movement and changes. Roberts also highlights some differences between libraries during the 1970s and nowadays as '[n]othing was computerised at that point' or '[y]ou wouldn't dream of bringing in bottled water and taking regular sips' or '[m]obile phones, of course, did not exist' (21-2). History and progress are put down on the text with the reflective voice of the writer-protagonist.

Michèle Roberts's *Paper Houses* is a contribution to history from the protagonist's interior eyes with the meditative participation of her story and her observations of London's backgrounds. While *flâneur* implies a more rational, structured and purpose figure, the *flâneuse* is more informal, flexible, nomad and a lover of picturesque (Parsons 8). Roberts has focused on the 1970s and 1980s as a witness and equally as an actress who performed according to the situations presented (Roberts 6). In Parsons's words, '[t]he postmodern city is an open and migrational one, available to female as well as male walkers of the city street' (9). Roberts, on the contrary, have preferred to maintain the masculine term, the original modernist theory to adapt it into a female gendered being that enjoys more freedom as she lets herself go in the streets of London. Roberts's *flâneuse-flâneur* aims to combine modernism and postmodernism. As she said: 'She [the *flâneur*] doesn't particularly want to direct the traffic when she's out for a wander. She follows her nose. She follows her desire' (Roberts 6). Roberts's female *flâneur* is free will and flexible with no restrictions to walk any path she decides to take but she will do it from within.

This *flâneur* experience of wandering and walking in London and through different rooms and communal houses, between interior and exterior spaces, is also a way of travelling, continuity and of expressing herself by means of the heroine's journeys. Michèle Roberts not only uses the modernist form to embark on the writing of her memoir but she also revisits discovers her inner journeys now that she is a constructed woman and a prolific writer. Her voyage is one of freedom and exploration: 'Worry dissolved when I roamed London and forgot myself in exploring it' (74). As Parsons claims, '[w]alking in the city is at once an encounter with modernity and with the past, with the new and unknown but also with haunting ghosts' (10). Roberts's trip is to come across with her identity, which, on the one hand, had to deal with those ghosts in her psyche, and on the other hand, had to pursue being a writer. To become a woman and a writer is a process presented in the text through Roberts's walk, through Roberts's writing. Casey Blanton has acknowledged that when writing about travel writing: '[t]he reverberations between observer and observed, between self and world, allow the writer to celebrate the local while contemplating the universal' (5). In the case of Roberts's memoir, the local is her interior and her cultural background is the city. The universal is represented by the historical events that are combined with her personal actions. By associating personal and public accounts, Roberts shares experiences with other noteworthy men and women of her living time. Roberts has lived a revolutionary historical period in one of the most urban settings in the world: London.

In cultural terms, Roberts's exploration is also a panorama to observe together with the memoirist's understanding of what the city, the time and the people are like in London. This cultural environment allows the contemporary reader to visit and revisit the 1970s and 1980s from a new perspective of journeys of rediscoveries that is focused on language and content. The 1970s and 1980s in London become then familiar for the native reader and the foreign reader, being a non-British reader or someone who has not experienced London the way Roberts tells in her autobiography. Foreigner here does not only have cultural implications but it also becomes other than Roberts's account. This is her story and it is unique but, at the same time, it participates in the history of London and in the movement of feminism. The universal account referred to by Roberts is what native and foreign may share with this writer. The rest is single and private to her. Roberts's cultural language and content are thus produced in *Paper Houses*.

Regarding the *flâneur* experience, travellers also allow a subject and object relationship between an observer and an observed person. When dealing with the *flâneur*, there is a union of binaries between present and past, history and story, interior and exterior. Casey Blunton suggested that 'whether fiction or non-fiction, there exists in the journey pattern the possibility of a kind of narrative where the inner and outer worlds collide' (3). In *Paper Houses*, the perception of the *flâneur* differs from that of the traveller because the stroller lives the streets and the cultural experience as part of her identity while the traveller is a short term visitor who may have nothing to do with the described culture. Although Roberts is the contemporary, female *flâneur* that explores a conflict between personal and public, this contraposition disappears when both selves finally live together by accepting each other.

Paper Houses is a story created by memory and invention. In other words, Roberts has shaped this fictional and real story by rereading and rethinking about the protagonist's past with a present and more mature perception. It is by means of writing this memoir that Roberts looks into her past and that the importance of writing from external surroundings becomes vital in the construction of her identity. King argues that 'assumptions about the nature of memory shape not only notions of personal identity but also the relationship of culture to its past, and the nature and structure of the narratives that reconstruct the past' (King 28).

One can also see *Paper Houses* as fictional autobiography combined with some features of travel writing. Roberts's memoir 'borrows from the world of fiction to establish motivation, rising and falling of action, conflict, resolution, and character' (Blanton 4). In both cases, travel literature and autobiography need of an individual consciousness, being female and feminist in Roberts's account. As 'the literature of modernity has been impoverished by ignoring the lives of women' (Wolf 205), Roberts's *Paper Houses* celebrates the personal life of the writer-protagonist who becomes a heroine, a modern female *flâneur* and a postmodern *flâneuse*.

The modern female *flâneur* or the postmodern *flâneuse* of *Paper Houses* looks into her inner world in order to find a correspondence to the outer world. The following episode is especially devoted to *Paper Houses* as a memoir that combines personal and public accounts in the same literary text.

Paper Houses: a woman's fictional memoir

A memoir is part of an autobiographical text in which the writer's main aim is to focus on political matters rather than personal issues. The principal purpose of a memoir is to present in words some selected historical time that the memoirist has lived in. Most memoir writers have been male politicians and military people. However, feminist writers have also had a say and have supplied content to this literary form which aims for a balance between personal and public.

Kristi Siegel portrays a research study on the beginnings and evolution of the autobiography for women writers. Her book, *Women's Autobiographies, Culture and Feminism*, illustrates different examples of autobiography as a writing form that was taking shape for women as well. Yet, this female autobiography will be different to that written by men. As Siegel points out, 'women's autobiography is distinguished by its uneasy relationship to the body and maternity' (12). In her analysis, Siegel highlights three methods used by women autobiographers, as suggested by Norrine Voss: 'archaeological studies, studies in groups of autobiographies possessing a common trait; and studies centering on the subject of 'difference', that is on how women's autobiographies differ from men's' (12-3).

Michèle Roberts's *Paper Houses* can be grouped into Siegel's third classification because Roberts's writing aims to be altered from the imposed, omnipresent techniques developed by men. As Roberts points out, from a present and conscious standpoint, her writing, although conventional and masculine at the beginning, started to be influenced by spiritual writers of mystical authorities: 'I trusted abstract reasoning less than thoughts that came out of my own experience in the world and from my own inner side. Poetry and novels arose from very deep down inside' (278). Roberts aimed not for 'the words of conventional grammar which separated things but the words of poetry which recombined them' (279). In *Paper Houses* the feminist writer acknowledged her initial need for authoritative, traditional and mainly, male writing. Later on her writing formation changed in a subversive way. Roberts has always intended to put her body and language down in her text. It is the latter which symbolises the body of her text and vice versa. As she continued: 'we are not separate from the world but part of the world's body' (279). This union between content and form is what women's writing is about. If male writing aims to separate theory and practice, female writing proposes the combination of both with a clear, distinctive, female voice.

Furthermore, Roberts embarks upon writing her memoirs by using different sources. She has been rereading her diaries and her written records of personal and political events happening in the1970s and 1980s in London and she has also used her memory to travel through her inner and outer past. Roberts has even bumped into photos of her young, revolutionary time in London. Although Roberts has tried to be truthful to the lived facts and how she saw and remembered them, she also confessed that '[t]his memoir is like fiction, in as much as I have shaped and edited it' (Roberts 7). Roberts is intertwining her personal life and what she remembers with some invented situations that are not so true, at least, not in her mind. These combinations between reality and fantasy, between history and story form her personal account, *Paper Houses*.

At the same time, Roberts's memoir focuses mainly on the urban place of London, the city that has evolved with her personality, her identity and her writing. Each of the chapters has the name of a neighbourhood or a park, mostly in London, and a photo of Roberts's friends or herself together with an explanatory line during such personal and controversial decades in the English capital. Roberts has genuine material such as her diaries and her photos to shape her memoir and to make it more real to the reader. The temporal setting of Roberts's text starts just after she had finished her university studies at Oxford and once she moved to London. Although there are two chapters entitled Bangkok and Cambridge, Massachusetts, London is the paramount location chosen by Roberts to write her memoir and thus to (re)create her identity as a woman and as a writer.

Roberts subversively acknowledges the statement written by Woolf by connecting her personal and professional experiences with that of the Victorian writer. Both writers highlight the importance of writing as women and of moving freely as female *flâneurs* that will deal with solitary and crowded spaces simultaneously. As suggested by Woolf, Roberts identifies that she does not have a room of her own, a place of her own. While she was living at home, she used to share rooms with her sister and, at college, with university mates. That individual and personal place Virginia Woolf had already proposed was not part of Roberts's environment. Roberts, nevertheless, begins this process of individuality, of discovering herself. The first important step is to construct her identity by facing difficult situations alone. As she confesses on the first chapter: 'For the first time in my life I was on my own' (14). Not only will this independent time be the beginning of her identity but of all her personal conflicts. The historical movements Roberts lived in such remarkable time also contributed to form her identity. In *Paper Houses*, Roberts will be alone but also in groups of friends, intellectuals, feminist activists, indoors and outdoors. The young protagonist 'is another alienated figure in the city, an outsider struggling to maintain independence in the submerging crowd' (Parsons 50).

In the opening chapter of *Paper Houses*, Roberts deals with individuality, religion, sex, demonstrations, family, profession, feminism, books, and writing. Above all, the contemporary writer connects with her past being and portrays her intention from a present perspective: 'She intends to become a writer, is determined to publish a novel before she is thirty, and she expects to be poor' (15). Social and professional revelations are projected on these initial pages. This dialogue between Roberts's past and her present conscious narrative of that earlier period are clearly revealed on this same page when Roberts breaks the *she* subject narrator down and transforms it into the *I* voice again: 'Yes, I was unrealistic in my would-be bohemian, she says to me: but at least I had ideals. And in my own muddled way I did get involved in radical politics. It's all right, I shout back at her: I'm not here to judge you' (15).

Although the feminist writer follows a chronological setting from the 1970s onwards, the content of Roberts's account starts in the

1970s. There is a frequent inner journey that continues up to today's time while her memoir narrative style finishes after she and Tim got divorced, her personal account, and after *Flesh and Blood* was published, her professional account. On the other hand, Roberts goes backwards and forwards in her narration letting her unconscious and conscious mental states take part in the story. She listens to her inner voice to reflect upon political issues. As Roberts has remarked, although she tried to follow a chronological order when telling her events, her memoir also goes in circles: 'It circles around different images and themes, runs back and forth between inner and outer worlds, loops between sketches of thinking, dreaming and writing, and sketches of culture' (6).

The personal combines the professional side in this representation of Roberts's life. The writer participates in her own text by telling her private story and by including whereabouts, places and times that do not only belong to her confidential tale but to the public history. As Roberts said, the connection between personal story and public history is as necessary in the construction of her identity as it is the creation of writing: 'I take my past with me. History matters. The continuity remains: the relationship continues to evolve and change, while our artists' bond stays as strong as ever' (337).

Paper Houses: A Memoir of the '70s and Beyond combines public and personal selves being the focal starting period the 1970s in London. The public history and the literary culture are thus portrayed in Roberts's personal history. We get to reflect upon Michèle Roberts's journal and previous notes and to know anecdotes which have been previously experienced by the writer who is also protagonist of her text. There are some conscious examples that go deep inside the character's mind and feelings. One of them is describing how Roberts observes this girl of the 1970s from a present viewpoint. The memoirist declares: 'She writes her diary so self-critically, suffers so much, berates herself so harshly for suffering and then for writing about it ... She wants adventures. She has come to London, in the time-honoured way, to have them' (14). In *Paper Houses*, Roberts makes a conscious observation about herself, the

1970s and 1980s, and London. Roberts is travelling in her mind and in her city because she is not rooted. She is more 'like a *flâneur'*, like 'someone displaced' (Parsons 60). The protagonist has developed experiences in a radical London with continuous demonstrations for the rights of women. Roberts's handwritten diaries, her conscious inner thoughts, her reflection on the political and historical matters, and her imagination have been essential elements to create the fictional memoir of *Paper Houses* and to be the woman and the writer she is today. Roberts's participation in autobiographical writing allows her to become the heroine of her own text and life. Revisiting her diaries and her conscious and idealised past allows Roberts to build on her identity as a woman and as a writer. As Spencer argues, autobiography was a mode used by women writers as it:

> [S]uited women because in it they could become their own heroines, and as we have seen the cultural association between heroine and woman writer was strong. Romanticized autobiography, or fantastic fiction starring an idealized version of the author, provided a means not just of self-projection but of creating one's identity and authority as a woman writer. (Spencer 41)

Michèle Roberts's personal and public *Paper Houses*

> All narrative accounts of life stories, whether they are the ongoing stories which we tell ourselves and each other as part of the construction of identity, or the more shaped and literary narratives of autobiography or first-person fictions, are made possible by memory. (King 2)

Memoirs and autobiographies, together with travel writing accounts are written in the *I* voice, '[b]eing both identical when it is political and unique when it is personal' (Smith 8). In each of these narrative compositions, memory takes its part and it is by means of the protagonist-writer's recall and perceptions of episodes that the story is putting down. Memoirs, autobiographies, travel writing and the feminist novel have some features in common as they tell the story from the observer's perspective with some personal interpretation of the writer. Although the novel is mainly described as a fictional work, the other three narrative styles aim to be true to reality. An autobiography usually implies a longer text comprising the complete life of the writer, while a travel writing account tells the story of the traveller from a foreigner's perspective. A memoir, on the other hand, needs of the memoirist's recollection of data to get the story from a particular period of time rescued and told. The novel is centred on a work of fiction that is not real, but compared to the autobiography or travel writing, the feminist novel also highlights the importance of using the first person narrator. It is the inside voice of the protagonist of the feminist novel that confesses her personal account to the public audience what the feminist novel shares with Roberts's memoir. With all this in mind, I would like to analyse the structure, process and final creation of Michèle Roberts's memoir, her paper house. I will also study some similarities among the memoir, the feminist novel and travel writing. There are two journeys happening simultaneously while dealing with Roberts's *Paper Houses*: first, we get to know the historical, cultural and personal evolution of the protagonist, and second, we participate in the creation of *Paper Houses*, which is the final production of Roberts's autobiographical account. In this regard, it will be vital to deal with the terms gender, culture and place in order to understand the individuality and multiplicity of *Paper Houses*.

In *Paper Houses, A Memoir of the '70s and Beyond*, Roberts acts as the writer who is now conscious about her past experiences and about the relationship between her past and present times. In this regard, although the writer aims to be true to the events, the story plays with characteristics distinctive of fiction. It is the first person narrative together with the other, being the world, other women, men, children society, religion and culture what Roberts's memoir points out in her memoir. Sidonie Smith adds: 'As integuments of subjectivity, memoirs are so many umbilical cords connecting the narrator to the swirl of others surrounding her' (97). The subject of the text is the body of the text itself looking inwards and outwards at the same time. The voice telling Roberts's story-history engages in an introspective mode which requires that the events are shared with the external world. In addition, Smith has claimed that '[d]iscourses of embodiment also mark woman as an encumbered self, identified almost entirely by social roles concomitant with her biological destiny' (12). In Roberts's memoir, her present voice recalling and valuing past experiences that were constructing her identity is reflected by the relationships she maintained with her inner self and with others in physical, social and psychological circumstances. It is very recurrent to observe images and conversations of Roberts with other feminists of her time. Below, there is a clear example of this combination between personal story and public history related to the feminist movement:

> I enjoyed attending a women's college. I liked being part of a community of women who took each other seriously as equals. Women formed the centre of this world. (16)
> Falling in love with feminism, I was falling out of love with the Library. (35)
> Being a Real Woman as achieved by laborious art; a sort of transvestism. We defined femininity as a performance and dramatised it in the street. (47)

Being a woman dealing with body and intellectuality, feminism and politics meant being revolutionary during the 1970s in London. The protagonist and writer of her own account had to face personal and political conflicts in order to survive and consequently, find her identity. As Roberts suggests in the introduction of her memoir: 'I prepared for my new life, post university, in London, by buying a notebook, a midi-skirt (after years of minis it felt daring to conceal one's leg)' (11). From these very first lines, the writer exposes her purpose at the time of writing this personal and fictional account by making reference to her personal appearance and clothing, a topic concerning young women's minds. Even though Roberts participates in her writing as an individual, there are references to other women of her time. Roberts's memoir is both personal and collective. The two lines go together. Young Roberts is ready to start writing and to be in fashion so that she can start her new life in London. The author also introduces the setting and the time of her autobiography as characteristics that contribute to consider her memoir personal and distinctive.

The form of Roberts's memoir echoes the feminist novel as it mainly centres on plot and identity. There is continuity from one episode to the other and the reader participates in the heroine's evolution and experiences. Doris Sommer has already suggested that novels together with autobiographies complement the gaps of the official history. This revision of the past that Roberts pursues in her literary production is in a way, a process in which '[n]ovelists responded by constructing alternative versions of the past' (Sommer 116). Michèle Roberts has been working in this reconstruction of the past through her novels and now, through her memoir. Her memoir is also about the history of London, the history of the seventies and eighties and the history of feminism as a home for her. *Paper Houses* is also about the formation of a feminist woman that struggles to become a committed writer.

Nancy A. Walker has mentioned that after the long debate about the relation between art and reality, it has been after the 1970s 'when feminist critics began to posit that women as writers and readers participate in the creative process more directly than do men' (16). Roberts reflects on this critical feminism and this creative participation in *Paper Houses*. Mary G. Mason has also highlighted that 'the history of autobiography is largely a history of the western obsession with self at the same time the felt desire to somehow escape that obsession' (44). *Paper Houses* combines the feminist form of the novel with the autobiographical testimonies the woman protagonist-writer portrays in her text. It should be no surprise, however, to be expecting, at least as contemporary feminist readers, the link between autobiography and novel when dealing with a woman's identity. In *Paper Houses* the self is on stage. The self is being revised to put the body down. Roberts's current thoughts, although trying to be true to her memory are reshaped with some invented names or anecdotes, as the writer confesses. Roberts, the memoirist, is the protagonist of her personal account and the heroine of this real, literary work. Her private story is now part of the public history of London. Roberts's personal, social and political consciousness is a contribution to women's history in London during the 1970s and 1980s. The formation of Roberts's identity is now open to contemporary readers. Although 'strange', as she states, Roberts undertakes the mental conscious inspiration of writing a unique memoir, which, at the same time, shares common characteristics with other women stories:

> Writing this story joins up all the scattered bits of me, makes them continuous, gives me a conscious of self existing in history, a self able to make decisions ... I subsequently make this memoir, this story. I learned how to tell stories first of all through writing fiction; it feels strange to do that in autobiography. (6)

A memoir is not exactly the same than an autobiography as the latter usually comprises the complete life of the writer while the former centres on a particular period of time which uncovers the writer's life. A memoir is also characterised by being more emotional. This touching feeling connects the memoir and the feminist novel. Roberts, the current memoirist, recalls her past, particularly the 1970s and the 1980s, by rediscovering and facing very emotional situations that have become part of her identity: feminism, mother-daughter and father-daughter relationships, sex, love, friendship and religion, for instance. Memoirs, even true to the writer's memory, follow the pattern of storytelling with a plot, characters, setting, time and, occasionally, some fictional characteristics.

When dealing with *Paper Houses*, the link between memoir and travel writing is also part of this debate. I suggest that it is possible to put side by side Roberts's memoir with travel writing because the protagonist's performance is that of a female *flâneur*. As the author said: 'A journey, I discovered, was like writing: pushing into narrative. You had to invent it ... step by step' (104). *Paper Houses* is about two journeys: the physical and the personal. Roberts's body and mind are depicted to explore and to discover, question, accept and reject whatever the circumstances the protagonist will have to face. Roberts's memoir resembles that of the travel writing account in the sense that it tells the story of a particular period of time and in a particular place by the traveller or stroller. However, the travel writer is usually a foreigner, an outsider of the location while in Roberts's memoir the protagonist belongs to the place, the traditions, the language and the culture. Roberts knows London and as a native citizen. She is able to explore its streets, its people, its shops, its buildings, its parks, its houses and its history. As Roberts argues, the 1970s and 1980s decades in London were crucial for the women's liberation movements and it was due to those demonstrations, and due to other personal and family concerns that Roberts's personal and professional identity was celebrated: 'The first London demonstration for women's liberation took place on Saturday 6 March, 1971, to coincide with International Women's Day. About two thousand women, children and supporting men turned up and turned the day into carnival' (38).

There is a chronological vision of Roberts's memoir as well as a focus on her course to become a writer and an independent woman with a home of her own. The two journeys seem to happen simultaneously in *Paper Houses*. Roberts embarks on her commitments to turn into a writer and the feminist and activist woman she was then and she is today. It was actually by means of writing that Roberts found her goal during such a controversial historical period: 'Writing was my soul-saver. Like so many other young women, I had to rebel' (55). We get to discover the arguable seventies from a personal, political and feminist perspective. Michèle Roberts's memoir contributes to preserve history by including the author's personal experiences. Roberts's feminine consciousness pursues to become a writer under whatever circumstances such as being poor and her parents' disappointment, for instance: 'I could not imagine how to become an artist within the parameters of my strongly Tory and religious family. I had grown up, thanks to Catholicism, fearing my own body' (54-5). The young protagonist stresses the message of fighting back and continuing as a woman and as a feminist.

The main character of *Paper Houses* feeds her personality through different journeys of consciousness and reflection. One passage is related to Roberts's upbringing and religious background. Her original personal environment was contrary to her changing freedom, and to her purposes of becoming a critical writer who freely says what her body and mind want to express. Consequently, the protagonist had to resist various 'Mother Superiors' who were confining her dreams and body. Religion, in particular Catholicism, is in this regard one of the subject matters Roberts had to deliberately fight back. Catholicism is a recurrent topic in Roberts's writing, as the writer needed to resist, survive and become a liberated woman in her body and mind: 'The Catholic Church taught that a single woman could not be both holy and sexual. Why not? Why did a woman have to split in two?' (248).

The purpose of Roberts's memoir is introduced on its first page: 'This memoir begins at the point when I left university and came to London, and tells of my adventures there, in a wide range of districts and streets and a succession of flats and houses' (3). Roberts describes her experiences highlighting her journeys, her participation at communal and individual houses and her moving anecdotes from one house to the other as fundamental actions in the creation of her identity and her writing. As Roberts stresses, she was 'zigzagging between inside and outside' (3) and the seventies gave her a liberal formation, a new way to live her life (5) and to become the woman and the writer that she is today.

Roberts shares with other nineteenth century and contemporary feminist writers, the need to combine her personal story with political, critical and public history. In this line, the 1970s gave her the revealing experience because 'discovering that personal life, domestic life, formed part of politics' (49). As a woman writer living in such an exciting and historical period for feminism, Roberts had to defy these personal and political spheres in order that they could be rethought and modified. She quotes relevant feminist intellectuals such as Adrienne Rich, Jean Rhys and Germaine Greer who contributed to focus on the personal rather than the public. *Paper Houses* deal with the personal touch but this time the protagonist is called Michèle Roberts. Her previous experimental writing and her story telling techniques have given her the language needed to write this autobiographical text of a particular period of her life. Even though

Roberts was not consciously acknowledged as an experimental writer, she reconsiders and asserts it herself when positioning at the time of publication of *A Piece of the Night* (158-59). As it occurred with her novels, her memoir is about putting the body down and about combining the internal and the external sides: 'I saw the text as a body that had been cut and damaged' (159). As a female *flâneur*, Roberts provides different examples of that connection between the streets of London and her inner place, being her home and her inner self. She needs both the outside and the inside to shape her identity: 'When I got home at four o'clock I felt the outside come in with me. My room felt light and blowy' (142).

The content of *Paper Houses* corresponds to its form. As a woman's autobiographical text, the development of the *I* voice is recurrent and highlighted in Roberts's text. Sidone Smith has declared that '[a]ll 'I's are ontologically identical, rational beings – but all 'I's are also unique. This is the stuff of myth, imperious and contradictory' (8). Initially, the solitary voice, presented in women's autobiographical writing, aims to tell the individual story of that exclusive woman in question. However, it is remarkable to say that some characteristics of the individual psyche are shared by other women. The private life acknowledges public states. Thus, the individual *I* shares common situations, perceptions, content and language with other unknown but public *I*s.

In the case of Roberts's memoir, this writer has been selective when choosing either *I, we* or *she* and *they*. The *I* is the private story. This is *me* and my voice opposed to *we* who implies that the author has taken part in that narrative not as an individual but as a member in a commune, in a group. *She* and *they* are, on the other hand, represented as part of Roberts's memoir. *She* and *they* are the nutrients of Roberts's personal construction. These other events and personalities are described as communities, families or singular people and friends who are also part of Roberts's memories. They belong to Roberts's account. They are not separated from her own private and reflective story. These third person characters are secondary protagonists but they have contributed to the creation of Roberts's memoir because they were publicly there. Yet, the gazing eye of the writer makes these other voices participative in Roberts's story. These third person subjects are objects of the present, conscious narrative. In the following lines, there is a communal message of principles: 'We believed in passionate sexual love between men and women, as equals. Men were our brothers and comrades, even when we fought them' (67). In *Paper Houses*, *We* usually corresponds to the public, the exterior world in which Roberts was positioned while the *I* voice corresponds to the writer's inner feelings presented in a confessional form: 'I fantasised about becoming a revolutionary librarian' (67). The third person subjects of Roberts's sentences portray the historical events as in: 'The miners' strike was happening, and the government had declared a state of emergency' (70). First and third person voices are united in this piece of writing to create a memoir about Roberts's life and writing during her early years in London. The personal and the historical accounts gather to form Roberts's memoir.

As Helen M. Buss has suggested, the memoir 'is a form in which one cannot rely only on the facts of official history, yet it is a form in which one cannot dispense with historical narrative ... yet it is a form in which one must suspect one's sources, doubt them while affirming them' (xiv). Memoirs are about binaries. The twofold world of trusting and questioning one's own sources and one's own memory serves as a structure for Roberts's account. Both history and fiction are intertwined in the narrator's mind. The protagonist connects with her past and with her other self in order to construct a historical narration that it is also combined with fiction and autobiography. London and her personal experiences gave Roberts that practical new writing of a secreted history, the history of the gaps. Roberts point out that there were 'class groups to write and publish a new sort of history, a new sort of autobiography: the lives of ordinary people' (132).

Ramona Wray in her analysis of autobiographical texts in Early Modern Women's Writing, edited by Laura Lunger Knoppers argues that 'some memoirs employ strategies more commonly associated with the novel, others take on qualities that show a greater affinity with the biography' (199). Roberts's memoir associates both techniques. As a researcher and as a writer, Roberts has maintained some original techniques from her early modern women predecessors but it is not questionable that the historical account this writer-protagonist experiences differ from her past women writers. The emphasis on women's autobiography and the dialogue between personal and public accounts are characteristics maintained by this contemporary memoirist. As Roberts's content is singular and it happens in a more liberated period than the early modern women writers, form is also adapted. Her literary works represent some of Roberts's inner voices and also, her need to invent and construct a self. It has been through writing *Paper Houses* that the writer-protagonist has constructed her space for reflection, where she deals with her thoughts, fears and forms of her identity: 'I put all my anger into my diary; my paper house: my paper cupboard. Writing contained and shaped unacceptable feelings' (253).

Roberts's memoir is a rewritten composition of her reality back then in the seventies but with present conscious allegations about her young personality. This current conscious and mature voice recalls a past of fantasy, adventures, sex and independence. In the following lines, Roberts describes controversial moments of her protagonist. The writer expresses her existing feelings for her young heroine. Time is presented as a borderline but also as a link between the two selves: 'I do feel sorry for that younger self. She was plummeting towards rock-bottom. Why on earth shouldn't I pity her? I couldn't do it then. I would berate myself: come on! Get up! Cope! Probably just as well. I did keep going' (230). Roberts depicts the personal circumstances of her protagonist and aims to rescue her by writing her story. Personal difficulties, lonely situations plus money uncertainties, together with the contentious historical period lived, were part of Michèle Roberts's emancipation.

Although emancipation for Roberts was linked to writing, one of the recurrent topics women writers have criticised by means of the novel is marriage. It was the only domestic life and profession that women were approved to maintain. As Nancy Walker has argued:

> Contemporary women novelists, aware of the effect of fictions (both literally and cultural) on themselves and their readers, also write cautiously tales, but they subvert the marriage plot. Their characters leave marriages and refuse them all together; they have affairs and do not drown themselves or turn on the gas; they seek identity in work, their friends, and themselves rather than primarily in men. (Walker 16)

Roberts, heroine and writer of her own personal account, is aware of the power of predictable plot and moves between history and fiction in the journey of uncovering her identity. *Paper Houses* also depicts an implicit critique to marriage and it is certainly not the nurturing need for the creation of Roberts's identity. However sexually emancipated, the writer-protagonist chooses to marry twice, once with William, an academic scholar in December 1983, and about ten years later with Jim, an artist.

Roberts's first marriage was more conventional with clearly distinctive roles between husband and wife. Roberts was lacking her writing time and space. With Jim, on the other hand, Roberts clearly shows how much in love she is with her husband. As she says in *Paper Houses*: 'I loved sharing his space and I was in love with him and that desire and pleasure fed straight into my writing' (312). Roberts's happy and emotional state is a constructive consequence in her fruitful literary production. She is, as Nancy A. Walker will put bit, 'starting over' (11). This new beginning is not only observed in her new personal life, or in other words, in the content of Roberts's life, but also in the form of *Paper Houses*. As Walker continues: 'the lives of many of the narrators and characters in contemporary fiction by women is represented in the multiple narrative perspectives that so many of these writers use' (11). With Jim, the protagonist could continue with her creative life while with William, she was mostly attached to domestic life without much time for individual exploration: 'Fulfilling the man's needs left less time for writing' (247).

Being married to William silenced Roberts both in the private and public scenes. As they moved and lived in Italy, language was another drawback the protagonist had to face as she did not speak Italian. So, it was not only a new married life condition, but also the location and the language what depressed Roberts very much. While William was an exceptionally charming and intellectual academic, she was the wife who became only active while preparing parties and food for William's university colleagues. This new role was like hell for her as she had lost her independence. Her identity is only recognised by means of William's name. As Roberts declares: 'Without language, I felt completely invisible and that I did not exist (and anyway who was this Signora Binns? I did not know her). Also, I became cut off from politics' (243). Roberts's current conscious voice asserts that as a young, married woman she did not have a first name. As a married woman, the protagonist was someone else's wife, with someone else's surname. She was William's wife. That was it. Roberts did not take much political and social advantage of her first marriage as it quickly silenced and concealed her. The way Roberts was living with this popular scholar was very conventional. William's background represented the male academia which was not very positive about the position of women as feminists or intellectuals.

Although Roberts's economic strength was improved during her years with William, she lost her public role as a professional writer and feminist activist. As she argued in her memoir, being a wife was a performing act she had to learn. Roberts had to struggle with her inside, being wild and in need of discovering her persona and, her outside, being a well/ behaved companion: 'Wife! The word didn't suit me at all. I tried hard to carry out my side of what seemed a bargain, to behave appropriately, to appear a grown-up *signora*, but inside I was still a wild girl, a hooligan, a messy boy, an amazon. In disguise' (244-45). This conventional marriage did not convince Roberts as she felt concealed from the world. As she declared: 'I ignored my inner voice and my friend's voice and went ahead', possibly because '[m]arriage would take [her] not only to Italy but into security' (236).

Jim, on the other hand, was the lover of her life. The marriage with Jim did not follow any conventional rules. Roberts was not only in love with Jim but both artists could share and live together as equals. As the heroine of *Paper Houses* consciously states, it was Jim the first man who acknowledged her as an artist: '[H]e [Jim] was the first man who had loved me as an artist and thought it was normal I should be one' (310). Jim provided Roberts with language and happiness. When writing about her passionate relationship with Jim, the memoirist feels like a young girl again with a full world open to her. When describing life with not yet her second husband, Roberts talks about language, creation, sex, daydreaming: 'I felt as though I were sixteen, just out the convent, kicking up my heels for the first time, and I felt worldly and womanly and sexually confident' (293). With Jim, the protagonist has also returned home, after her stay in Italy and America. She feels rooted again and the setting gives her the necessary confidence to fulfil her personal and professional identity. With Jim, young Roberts feels active and not trapped into an empty life. She is moving forward again. She feels like 'just wanting to be on the move' (294). Now that Roberts is back in London, she will continue strolling through new streets to feel the urban space. Exploring London's streets by herself makes the protagonist revalue the importance of a new beginning, of feeling herself sexually completed and happy: 'Sex makes the city fizz and spark ... The city writes itself into you, around you, on to your skin' (294).

Although the writer lived two very dissimilar marriages, matrimony is not the required condition to form Roberts's identity. On the contrary, Roberts portrays from the very first episode that free love is a more positive and superior option to that of marriage which she values as more degrading and negative. Not only love and the discovery of her sexuality will be advantages to shape Roberts's identity but also friends, professional writing and family. The protagonist subversively deals with a recurrent topic in women's novels by narrating her story as a wife, and by illustrating other possibilities of being a woman.

Roberts also deals with sex, one of the concerns she had to face by rejecting her religious upbringing: 'Though I wrote and dreamed about sex, I couldn't imagine actually going to bed with anyone' (17). For Roberts, her sexual emancipation started after her first relationship. Although her first sexual experience was not what she had expected, she was 'relieved' to be sexually active and to be able to explore her body from that moment on. As she continued: '[A]t least, I got rid of my virginity' (26). From now on, the revolutionary protagonist is sexually liberated and her body gains recognition in her own psyche. The young Roberts does not reject her body any more, as her Mother Superiors used to command her. She is being transformed into a new woman who is sexually free, socially urban and with different jobs and social status to be able to wander the streets on her own. In this line, language is also relevant when dealing with Roberts because language gives form to her content even though she has strived to find the right expressions and the precise combination of terms that are able to describe the experiences she has lived in:

> Much of my powerful self-assertion, my appetite for life and experience, converted itself into energy for writing, struggling with language, repeatedly diving into the unconscious to find new forms, new stories, new meanings for words. I didn't see writing as a substitute for living but somehow it made living possible. I lived freely in reading and writing. (217)

The union between language and form are vital in Roberts's literary production. Roberts has depicted her novels and her memoir by means of the proper language that represents her inside: 'I named and listed my treasures and put these words into my writing' (262). The unconscious becomes the necessary state that Roberts requires in order that she can search and create new meanings and, accordingly, new stories. This darkness corresponds to her inner world, with the psyche of the protagonist-writer. The unconscious is private and singular but it will also imply public and collective principles. The unconscious inner self is the free space where the writer-protagonist goes deep inside in order to be liberated and start writing. As Roberts argues: 'Creating happens in a kind of dreamy darkness, in which one is, paradoxically, as alert and focused as possible' (280). Roberts needs to look into her personal self in order to start writing as a woman.

The structure of Roberts's memoir: locations, anecdotes and form

As it has been stated in previous chapters, the dominant scenery for Roberts's personal account is the city of London. This temporal point of departure takes place just after being a university student at Oxford during the 1970s. London is therefore the focal location in the construction of Roberts's identity. Although this feminist writer is also linked to French locations, London will provide Roberts with journeys, both external and internal, to create her identity as a fulfilled woman and as a professional, feminist writer. In this chapter, I will present first the structure of *Paper Houses*, which is always introduced by at least a visual and personal photo, and a note below it. Second, I will study the locations that contributed to Roberts's transformation into an independent woman and writer. Finally, I will dedicate a few pages to the form and the content of *Paper Houses*, which, in a way, aim to complement the previous chapters of this second part dedicated to Roberts's memoir.

London is not only the scene for this personal and political account to occur but it is also the place to shape Roberts's personality, her insight and also her profession, which is the outer correspondence and the public side of her writing. In this regard, Whitword suggests that '[m]oney economy and the dominance of the intellect are intrinsically connected' (184). In *Paper Houses* Roberts tackles her own discovery by inventing her self, an identity which is a new and a repeated self at the same time (Sommer 119). In this journey, the writer deals with money and intellect with regard to a woman writer. This creation of a heroine who is living the modern city is initially an experience described only by men and 'their transformations in the public world' (Wolf 1985: 199). Michèle Roberts, however, does not describes her autobiography as one that it is only egocentric and looks into her lived moments as a young woman but she also looks at the world that surrounds her. This feminist writer combines her personal story, which deals with family, friends, lovers, jobs, food, shopping and social and political events, with the historical time she has lived in. This combination between history and fiction, between public and personal is manifested in *Paper Houses*.

The image that accompanies the introductory section of *Paper Houses* is Michèle Roberts's Library card from the University College of London. The introductory photo and the title of the chapter correspond to the chronological content dedicated to Roberts's life. Underneath Roberts's library card, it reads: 'My student card for Library School' (1). Roberts's election of this image to accompany the content of the introduction of *Paper Houses* is remarkable as it sets up not only this chapter but it defines the main topics of this personal account: women as bodily human beings and women as intellectuals. In this line, Roberts chose London and The British Library Card as symbols to start her journey of adventures. The city and the world of books participate in the construction of her identity.

Michael H. Whitworth has suggested that '[t]he city is the location where the more visible signs of modernity were to be found in the highest concentration' (2007: 181). London city is the place that allows the protagonist of *Paper Houses* to keep moving along with the historical period of time. Compared to the countryside, the city takes in more active events and mixed people who have opportunities to say what they want and to improve themselves. Michèle Roberts lived historical events in central London during her young age. In this regard, the historical moment, the city itself and Roberts's commitment to follow her bent and become a liberated woman and a writer are clearly described in this historical and personal memoir. Society became part of Roberts's reality and both were happening at the same time.

Chapters one and two are especially dedicated to moving around in central London with activist women friends during demonstrations regarding women's liberation. Regent's Park is the title of chapter one and there is a photo of Roberts and some other friends during the demonstration of March, 1971 with posters and a policeman riding his horse. The image portrays the trouble women had to face in order to achieve women's rights. Beneath the photo, Roberts refers not only to the demonstration mentioned but also to the Street-theatre group in which she used to perform as a feminist protester. Although chapter two moves a bit north to Holloway as the central location of this episode, the topic of feminism remains a focal subject in this second chapter as well. Under the photo of Roberts and other two friends, it reads: 'Sisterhood is powerful at the Women's Liberation conference in Skegmess, 1971'.

Clapham Junction is another place Roberts used to stroll about while moving houses in London. Now she is renting a room 'over a little terrace of shops' (73). The photo that accompanies the title of this second chapter is a photo of Roberts with short hair seating on the floor and smiling to the camera. The writing underneath the photo uses Roberts's French language influence and it reads: 'Chez Frances Wood, at St George's Square'. During this time, Roberts was having an affair with Terry, and even though he asked her to move in with him, she rejected the offer as she did not want to have any commitments. She rather preferred to feel sexually liberated: 'I wanted my independence. Part of that involved sexual freedom: I wanted to be able to sleep with other men' (73). While Roberts is roaming London, she walks around Vauxhall, Mile End Road, the East End, Pimlico and St George's Square.

Bangkok is the chronological location for chapter four as Roberts decided to apply for a job at the British Council in Thailand, where she was kidnapped on her arrival at the airport, suffered food-poisoning and was still questioning her personality, among other things. Even though she agreed to have this professional and cultural challenge in a foreign country, the protagonist did not cope either with the job or the cultural differences: 'I realised that my two lives were tearing apart. Neither of them corresponded to what I thought of as my 'true' self, whatever that was' (99). References to Roberts's identity are portrayed in this chapter as well, as she is performing a professional life that does not correspond to her personal life. As Thomas K. Fitzgerald pinpoints: 'It is culture that usually gives people their sense of identity whether at an individual or group level' (59). The coordinating conjunction *or* will be replaced by *and* in *Paper*

Houses because Roberts's identity will finally embrace that balance between individual and collective, between personal and public selves.

'Launch of 'A Piece of the Night', with Ruthie Petrie, Rosie Parker and Alison Fell' is the line presented below the picture of Roberts and other friends at the launch of her first novel. Chapter five combines the returning moment to London in 1973 that Roberts so much needed, together with the acknowledgement of her Nana being ill and her commitment to become a devoted writer. The personal and the public spheres are once again intertwined in this episode. Also, the protagonist describes what being a lesbian meant during that time. The emancipation and fulfilment as a writer are also considered in this episode: 'Writing meant voyaging into the unknown and having adventures; asserting myself and my capacity to tell tales' (109). Roberts connects once again the fact of being a woman, who deals with her sexuality and her personal life, with the fact of becoming a writer. That is her final purpose focal point in her memoir.

Chapter six opens with a photograph described as 'My Amazonian haircut' (151). Michèle Roberts's photo depicts a woman wearing a bath robe and handing a cup of tea. The principal London location is dedicated to Peckham Rye in the south. Roberts moved to a flat in that area with her lover Paula. This chapter is especially focused on Michèle Roberts's claim and celebration of being homosexual. This episode also deals with the heroine's inner, conscious and asserting condition of her identity. There are some events in which the protagonist celebrates her homosexuality: 'Loving another woman physically, coming with her, made me feel really good about being a woman for the first time in my life' (158). Yet, Roberts, from a contemporary perspective, consciously values her past sexual relationship with Paula as a nurturing need: 'I think, now, I tried, unconsciously, to turn Paula into a maternal figure (a good mother who pushed away that Mother Superior). She was older than I was. More experienced in life' (158). On the other hand, Roberts associated her personal experiences with writing. Paula provided Roberts with confidence and encouragement to publish her first novel. The current memoirist argues that the protagonist of the 1970s was exploring with writing and creation, between modernism and postmodernism. As she said, *Paper Houses*' heroine was dealing with modernist forms but she did not name them as such: 'you're a modernist' (158). She started from the practical form to finally identify what the theory of her writing style was about.

Holland Park is the title of chapter seven which is accompanied by three pictures of Portobello Market and Sarah LeFanu, a friend of Roberts. The house Michèle Roberts is sharing with Polly (the owner) and others in this chapter is offered to Roberts completely free and without a date to leave the property. This event is another reinforcement to encounter with her identity. This chapter also deals with family, money, friends and writing. In addition Roberts reflects on the position of the *flâneur* because the writer-protagonist conveys that *flâneur* was a behaviour only thought for men. Women were seen as 'street walkers' (187). Roberts criticises the position of men towards women during that time, as many did not appreciate what feminism was about and what the woman stroller meant. As an active eye-witness and as a liberal woman, Michèle Roberts is the female *flâneur* that does not need to transvestite to wander the streets of the urban space of London. Roberts brings up the case of remarkable George Elliot and some other women who cunningly found a way of emancipation and achievement during their historical time: 'How angry I felt with the men who curtailed my freedom to wander obliviously! I had no sympathy for them whatsoever' (186).

Chapter eight is entitled 'Notting Hill Gate' and it comprises Michèle Roberts's 'Holiday times with Duncan Campbell, Penny Valentine and Ros Asquith' (211). In this section three photos are depicting first, a couple, then, Roberts on her own and finally, Roberts with another friend. As in previous chapters, this episode is opened with references to her new place, her new home and her new paper house. This chapter is especially important because Roberts lives in a flat on her own for the very first time, a flat that she is able to organise and decorate by her herself: 'My compact little flat had two rooms, plus a tiny, doorless kitchen in an alcove with a curved outer wall, and a tiny bathroom' (213). As in previous chapters, the memoirist also puts her personal life down on paper. Roberts describes yet again her love and sex life. In this chapter, Roberts keeps moving forward and backwards with inner and outer reflections about her life, her identity, her emancipation as a free woman and as a proficient writer. She is now in the 1980s and her writing commitment is higher. The chapter finishes with her announcement of getting married to Robert. She will now dedicate her time to some domestic and married life that she has not considered before. She confesses that she has married to please others. The protagonist's testimony expresses that she has forgotten how to listen to her inside.

Although the title of chapter nine opens with a particular location, Bayswater, this episode deals with her personal experiences in Italy, especially in Rome, Florence and Venice. The title of this episode is accompanied by a photo of Roberts while performing and reading at *Angels of Fire*. This chapter highlights the protagonist's metamorphosis from an independent woman who did not look into domestic life to the wife who described the process of her marriage, the clothes, and her lack of space and time to think about herself. She is now a dedicated wife to her husband's needs. The heroine points up that she has ignored her independence and her political life. She completed, however, the novel of *The Wild Girl*, by having been reading and taking notes in libraries and by having visited churches and museums (247). There are also references to the *flâneur* when Roberts states 'What a difficult place Florence was to walk through!' (252). The protagonist of *Paper Houses* continues questioning the conception of having a home of her own. Roberts's home is a place where she can write. Writing feels like at home, and Florence did not give her the inspiration, place and time for writing: 'As a writer, I felt homeless in Florence' (255). Despite Roberts's difficulties to find the time and space for writing, *The Book of Mrs Noah* is acknowledged as a literary creation that the writer-protagonist fulfilled during her time in Italy (265).

Chapter ten is devoted to Roberts's time in Cambridge, Massachussets. The photo chosen to introduce this chapter is Michele Roberts's ID card of Resident Alien in U.S. At the bottom of the card, the writer has included the term 'displacement'. This episode is about facing her unsuccessful marriage and her sad reality and about finding a solution. Being in Italy gave her knowledge and private thoughts. After having gone back home for Christmas, she realised how much she had missed home, her country, her family and her friends. Nonetheless, Roberts decided to travel to North America to meet her husband who continued living an independent life by giving lectures at different universities. The masculine academic world is also criticised in this episode where Roberts confessed that she felt discriminated by the academia for being a woman: 'I loathed living in an institution. I loathed having to be polite all the time. I loathed the way most of the male academics did not bother speaking to me' (275). Following her husband's life did not suit the protagonist as she kept losing her space, her time with friends, her world and her identity. With this entire intellectual and personal atmosphere, Roberts is redrafting *The Book of Mrs Noah*, and is struggling to split language and body. She is aware of maintaining masculine traditional forms in her writing and she wants to change that because it does not correspond to her identity. This is one of the main themes she questions in *The Book of Mrs Noah*. As the memoirist said in *Paper Houses*, '[she] had to go away from that world of categories, into the freer space of poetry and art' (277). That switch is what she projects in *Mrs Noah*'s novel. This conscious separation between language and body allows her to speak up and transform her writing style into a more subversive form in which the long-established division between body and language is finally broken up in order that the writer becomes a more active and alive being: 'Writing the novel means that the dead body sits up on the bier and speaks' (280). The Arc created in *The Book of Mrs Noah* gave Roberts the words to travel around in 'the open sea' (282) and to discuss all possibilities of other women writers and men.

'Kitchen goddesses' and 'Teaching writing to City Lit students' are the two phrases that describe the photos which introduce chapter eleven, dedicated to Wivenhoe. Wivenhoe is a town in the borderline with Colchester in Essex, UK. During the late 1980s, Roberts spent some time in this county to become a playwright and to accomplish the job of Theatre Writer in Residence at Essex University. However, the heroine highlights that she felt lonely and that she continued being a female *flâneur* by walking the town she was living in: 'Walking induces rapture' (288). Roberts's awareness of her commitment to become a writer is once more portrayed in *Paper Houses* together with her inner battle to find the right words. Roberts has always intended to show her language, the language that has to do with her body, with her content: 'To find language I had to break down inherited forms of speech, destroy old grammars in order to construct new ones' (289). With the creation of Roberts's first play, *The Journeywoman*, she was also experimenting with language and with the construction of different pieces that were finally seen in a unit. She wrote consciously to unite body and language but she also suffered from seeing that her writing did not correspond to the interpretation of the play. Even though Roberts wanted the actors, the actresses and the audience to be aware of this union, she failed. That is the reason why she had to escape from Wivenhoe: 'Oh, the agony of seeing my baby having its fingers and toes chopped off!' (292). This chapter, however, finishes with a new beginning as Roberts meets up with her old friend Jim and they start a true love affair.

'Larking about with Jim' concludes the memoir of *Paper Houses* with photos of the cheerful lovers. The location that gives content to this chapter is Tufnell Park, an area in North London, which is near to Holloway and Regent's Park, the first two locations Roberts starting strolling at the beginning of her memoir. This chapter emphasises the circular movement of Roberts's language and content. The protagonist is now back home, back to her origins, back to the first place this story opened. It is in Tufnell Park and by living this romantic life with Jim that Roberts certainly confirms her identity. She used to live there about fifteen years ago. Now, Roberts is back to deal with family, love, sex, writing, walking, cooking and private spaces. *In the Red Kitchen* is the novel she is writing when she is living at Jim's and his ex-wife's house. This house was divided into two floors and into two lives. Roberts felt that this division was vital. The different parts of the house gave her the inspiration to start writing from the unconscious. On this occasion, *In the Red Kitchen* is based upon the life of the historical woman Florence Cook, named in Roberts's work of fiction 'the nineteenth century medium' (306). Roberts declared that Jim's house was 'a transitional space, neither up nor down but in between' (306). This link of binaries is repeatedly embodied by the protagonist of *Paper Houses*.

Below, I would like to present the outline of Roberts's memoir by including the titles of the chapters, the photos and the novels mentioned during this rediscovering process of writing her memoir and revisiting her identity. This layout is divided into two main sections. One is devoted to the chapters located in London and the other to the episodes placed outside London:

Chapters located in London

Introduction: Photo of Michèle Roberts Library Card: 'My student card for Library London'.

1. Regent's Park: The photo used to start this chapter presents Roberts in the Women's Liberation Demonstration in London in March 1971.
2. Holloway: Picture of Roberts and other friends at the Women's Liberation Conference in 1971.
3. Clapham Junction: Snapshot of Michèle Roberts on her own at her friends place, Frances Wood.
5. Camberwell: Photo of Roberts and some writing friends while her first novel *A Piece of the Night* was launched.
6. Peckham Rye: Individual Snaphot of Michèle Roberts entitled 'My Amazonian Haircut'.
7. Holland Park: Three photos, two of Sara Le Fanu and the last one of Portobello Market.
8. Notting Hill Gate: Three pictures of Roberts and his friends Duncan Campbell, Penny Valentine and Ros Agustin, while they were on holiday.
9. Bayswater: Photo of Roberts performing at Angels of Fire.
12. Tufnell Park: Two pictures of Roberts with Jim.

Chapters situated outside London and UK

4. Bangkok (Thailand): Two photos, the first, with Roberts and her friend Sarah Dunant and the second, a picture of Sue Maingay.
9. Bayswater: A photo of young Roberts performing at Angels of Fire. Although the title of this episode is Bayswater, I will include Rome, Florence and Venice because the story is especially developed in Italy. .
10. Cambridge, Massachussets (USA): Michèle Roberts's Resident ID Card.
11. Wivenhoe (in Essex, UK): Two pictures: one of sketches on Roberts's kitchen wall entitled 'Kitchen Goddesses' and the other, an image of Roberts teaching a writing course to City Literature Students.

> This shape aims to represent 1-6 zones of central London. The locations strolled by Roberts are numbered, according to the order they appear in *Paper Houses*.
>
>
>   12   2
>
>   9
>   1
>   8
>   7
>   3
>   5   6

Below, I have aimed to organise the novels written by Michèle Roberts mentioned in *Paper Houses* together with the year of publication and the page reference:

Novels by Roberts	Year of publication	Page number
A Piece of the Night	1978	p.180
The Visitation	1983	p.198
The Wild Girl	1984	pp.247-8, 256
The Book of Mrs Noah	1987	p.282
The Journeywoman premiered at Mercury Theatre, Colchester	1987	p.291
In the Red Kitchen	1990	p.306
Daughters of the House	1992	pp.313-323
Flesh and Blood	1994	p.334
Impossible Saints	1997	p.334

History and culture in London: the 1970s and 1980s

> The first London demonstration for women's liberation took place on Saturday 6 March, 1971, to coincide with International Women's Day. About two thousand women, children and supporting men turned up and turned the day into carnival. (*Paper Houses* 38)

This chapter is especially dedicated to the connection between history and culture with regard to Michèle Roberts's memoir and London. The quotation that introduces this chapter makes reference to historical and cultural events experienced by the real protagonist-writer of *Paper Houses*. Roberts had the vivid experience of taking active part in the first women's demonstration for women's freedom in London. Dates, locations and descriptive images are portrayed to help the reader visualise such imperative, historical and cultural events for women in England.

History is the discipline that studies the human past. Culture is a term that examines the individual and the group in a society that can be combined by different languages and lifestyles. Urban culture is especially devoted to what is happening in a town or city. London is a historical city that anyone can distinguish in its buildings, monuments, books, people, food and past events. The British capital has witnessed historical actions that authors such as Charles Dickens, Conan Doyle, Virginia Woolf, George Orwell and Edward Rutherfurd have described on paper. Many more writers have wanted to associate their content and form to the location of London.

In this line, Michèle Roberts has participated in the tradition of the urban culture and history by creating a memoir that it is placed in London, the city that has contributed to her formation as a woman and as a writer. Depicted in *Paper Houses: A Memoir of the '70s and Beyond* as a place for networking with the professional and the personal worlds, London is also the urban location for a woman to acquire freedom and especially, independence to move around. Michèle Roberts, the protagonist, is the woman who works on shaping her identity as a young woman in search for knowledge and in need of acceptance and emancipation. This powerful, historical and cultural London was the dual journey happening at the same time of Roberts's emancipation. *Paper Houses* is the personal narrative that makes references to historical and cultural London during the twentieth century from the perspective of a feminist woman writer.

One of the first instances that connect London to history and class is the cultural reference Roberts addresses when moving to a room near Regent's Park. The landlady of the flat the heroine was renting asked for a rental fee in guineas and not in pounds to preserve history and to stress her difference in social class status. As Roberts puts it: 'A guinea originally a gold coin, was worth one pound and one shilling. I felt abashed by Ernestine asking for guineas (not coined since 1813): they proved how upper-class she was' (13). This reference to the money she had to pay for her first individual room in

London was double the amount she had been paying in Oxford. Money is presented from the very first lines as an issue for the twentieth century protagonist who is committed to become a writer in spite of being poor (15). This context makes reference to Virginia Woolf's statement in her essay 'A Room of One's Own' in which money and writing as a woman used to be topics that could not be linked when one referred to women. Money is part of women's emancipation because they work and need financial resources to become independent and fulfilled women.

Roberts left her childhood home in 1967 to go to university in Oxford. *Paper Houses* is set after Roberts has finished her studies and starts living in London. London provides the young protagonist a room of her own for the very first time. Previously, she had to share rooms either at home or at college. Now in London Roberts shares a house with others but she starts having a private space for herself. Living in London implies being more independent as a young woman who is constructing her identity. Inner and outer spaces of London are presented in Roberts's memoir. The interior is in constant contact with the exterior.

The space of London is presented as a city that has had a meaningful influence on Roberts's literary production and identity. Likewise, the time the heroine has lived in London contributes to develop her persona. Feminism has given Roberts a home. It was stressed in *Paper Houses* that the 1970s and 1980s gave the protagonist time to demonstrate and to find relations of sisterhood and friendship with other women and with some men as well. Feminism is another recurrent cultural topic in *Paper Houses* because it contributed to cherish and support women as individuals and as a community: We believed in collective action and struggle. Our kind of socialism and feminism was idealistic and libertarian (46).

This community of women gave Roberts and other women of her time the necessary awareness to start talking about feminism. As women, they expressed that the personal was part of their political fight. As this writer states, '[n]obody thought of these as feminist subjects because we hadn't begun using those words' (16). Although Roberts lived a historical period of choice for women, she argues that they had to be in constant fight to maintain their freedom. It was due to a collective struggle that women acquired control over their lives. As Roberts continues: 'The pronoun mattered: we had the power to change our lives; we did not hang around waiting for leaders to turn up' (46). During the 1970s the personal and the pleasure of shaping women's identity were combined with the political and public spheres.

Feminism was consequently linked to the notion of being a woman. In *Paper Houses* Roberts makes reference to different feminists of her time who questioned the notions of feminism and womanhood. Irigaray is referred to when Roberts pinpoints what the notion of a girl and of a woman was at that time (49). Roberts also highlights that 'discovering that personal life, that domestic life, formed part of politics' (49). As Adrienne Rich has put it, the personal became the centre with regard to women's movements. This inner discovery and analysis of the woman's inside are journeys commonly portrayed in women's writing. Not only Roberts but other feminist writers have chosen this form of writing when expressing themselves in works of fiction, essays, plays, or any writing that has to depict the voice of the woman. Women were exploring their language and their body while they were writing fiction. With regard to the liberation movement, Roberts argues that:

> Being a Real Woman was achieved by laborious art; a sort of transvestism. We defined femininity as a performance and dramatised it in the street.
> Feminism could be carnivalesque and amusing. It could also disturb. Consciousness-raising, for example, let women meet together in small groups to talk confidentially about any subject we chose (47-8).

Feminism was a cultural passion in the 1970s in London. *Paper Houses* revisits those historical and cultural moments of exploration and performance that women had to face in a society dominated by men. Once women started looking into their interiors and participated in active demonstrations for their own rights did they come across with their real identities. Women realised that they had so much to say and to write about but language was limited. Women, such as Michèle Roberts, who have looked into their inner sides, their personal fears and happiness, wanted to explore and criticise political spheres but they did not have the proper words that could communicate with their own bodies. They had to invent a language that corresponded to their bodies: 'But how did you find the words to express your searches and your discoveries? They did not yet exist' (48-9).

There are constant examples of personal and historical events in Roberts's account. *Paper Houses* is about that bond between my story and history. Both narrations are happening at the same time and they do complement each other. Roberts's story belongs to the historical time she lived in London. The following example combines the miners' strike with Roberts's constant moving to other houses: 'The miners' strike was happening, and the government had declared a state of emergency ... I spent the night of 25 February 1972 crying while I packed bags and boxes' (70).

Religion together with sexuality is another cultural and historical topic intertwined not only in Roberts's novels but also in *Paper Houses*. As Roberts has always criticised in her work, the Catholic Church has divided women and has always diminished the position of women who have been negatively perceived as accepted bodies. According to Christians, women's body is to be limited, passive and repressed, especially with regard to sexuality:

> The Catholic Church divided women into evil temptresses or holy, sexless mothers. I had been taught that premarital sex was wicked, that adolescent sexual desires were wicked. Girls supposedly did not have desire, but had to control and prevent boys' desires. As a feminist I loved, desired and also resented men. I didn't believe in marriage, was fed up with men harassing me, thought I was anti-romantic, yet longed for a sexual companion (100).

Roberts has revisited Catholic narrations in order to search and discover new forms of being for women. Roberts's references to Catholicism have dealt with history and culture. The Church, society and politics have conditioned the position of women in history, society and religion. The repressed body becomes in Roberts's narration, on the contrary, an active entity that celebrates women's sexuality. *Paper Houses* participates in this celebration of the body with constant references to the flesh and sexuality with regard to women. This feminist writer has been haunted by the union between mind and body in search for the equality between men and women: 'Inside our tiny world, wholly centred on bed, we were equals, innocents, and there were no clichés. Adam and Eve dancing naked in the paradise garden; before the Fall' (101). The body is also memory and due to proper words the body can be expressed as language: 'For Woolf, a writer, and for most of us, visual memory can only be represented in language' (King 25-6). In *Paper Houses* Roberts has dealt with the particular and visual recollections of her inner memories together with past, personal and public events and the rereading of notebooks.

Michèle Roberts's body and language have portrayed her personal experiences as a woman and as a writer in historical and cultural London during the 1970s and 1980s with references to her personal and western background, upbringing and education. Thanks to writing, Michèle Roberts has found the words that can describe her inner sides, her language and her body. The feminist writer has lived between history and fiction, between reality and fantasy, between body and language, between sexuality and religion. Those binaries have shaped her writing style as a feminist woman whose identity as a twentieth century woman was born in London. Walking, exploring and combining her inner with her outer worlds gave Roberts the words to write novels, stories and histories which are presented in poems, novels, essays, plays and more recently, in the form of a memoir. Roberts has stated that writing is living. London has been the primary place to develop her personal and public lives:

> Alongside my novel I continued to write poetry and through poems I discovered a sort of language that let me live, the language of the body, expressed in metaphor. Metaphors connected the inner world to the outer world, opened them up to each other, connected conscious to unconscious. City could flow into self and self into city. That was how I experienced life, walking around. (141)

Index:
writers and historical women mentioned in *Paper Houses*

To conclude this section devoted to culture and history in urban London, I would like to present some intertextual references included in *Paper Houses*. Examples of historical events combined with personal moments have been already portrayed in this book. In this journey of past memories and reconstruction, Roberts walks around the city, travels through her mind and her diaries with references to other writers and activists that were acknowledged during the 1970s and 1980s in London. These cultural references form part of Roberts's memoir but they also belong to history. The following names and titles illustrate some of the reading references mentioned by Roberts in *Paper Houses*. These books and writers have contributed to the formation of Roberts as a reader and as the consequent writer that she is today:

The Bible (5)
Novels by Mauriac, Gide, Sartre and Lawrence (11, 139)
Shakespeare (11)
M. R. James's *The Apocryphal New Testament* (11)
English mystics: Richard Rolle, Margery Kempe and Julian Norwich (11)
Mechtild of Magdeburg (11)
Paradise Lost and Beowulf (11)
Simone de Beauvoir's *The Second Sex* (12, 69, 139, 264)
Georgette Heyer (13)
The Tale of Mr Jeremy Fisher (20)
Karl Marx (21)
Proceedings of the Society of Lady Book-Binders (25)
Le Blé en Herbe (26)
Lèvres de Velours (26)
The Other Victorians (26)
My Secret Life (26)
Fanny Hill (26)

The Story of O (26)
Nabokov's *Ada* (26)
Morning Chronicle (26)
The Politics of Experience (29)
Wanda (A Polish film, 30)
Mr Verdant Green Adventures of an Oxford Freshman (31)
Spectator (32)
Iliad (32)
Odyssey (32)
The Kinsey Report (33)
Mary McCarthy's *The Tynnary of the Orgasm* (33)
Katherine Whitehorn's *Cooking in a Bedsitter* (35)
Alma Tadema paintings (36)
Art in Revolution Exhibition (38)
Daniel Defore (43)
Mary Wollstonecraft (43)
Elizabeth Gaskell (43)
The Sensuous Woman by 'J' (48)
Cliff Richard and Mary Whitehouse (52)
Saint Teresa of Ávila (59)
Pamphlet called *The Tyranny of Structurelessness* (61)
Germaine Greer (67)
Kate Millet's *Sexual Politics* (69)
Frantz Fanon's *Black Faces White Masks* (69)
James Baldwin's *Giovanni's Room* (69)
Eagle and *Girl* (Comics for children, 76)
Doris Lessing's *The Four-Gated City, The Memoir's of a Survivor* (110, 216, 217, 224)
William Blake, (124)
The painter David Hepher (126)
Keats (126)
Marx and Engels (126)
Freud (127, 279, 319)
Tales I Tell My Mother (129)
Sara Maitland (139)

Emma Tennant (139)
Angela Carter (139, 227)
Emma (155)
Jean Rhys (174)
Colin MacInnes's *Mr Love and Justice* (174)
Julia Child's *Mastering the Art of Fresh Cooking* (178)
Press: *The Guardian* and *Time Out, The Daily Telegraph, Evening Standard* (186, 187, 197, 200, 203, 286)
Foucault, Lacan, Cixous (185)
Virginia Woolf (185)
George Sand (186)
The Woman in White (190)
Milton, D.H. Lawrence (198)
Marion Milner (219)
Michael Horowitz (222)
Frances Horowitz (223)
Fathers: Reflections by Daughters (230)
Jay Ramsay (231)
Virgil (233)
Beowulf (233)
Evelyn Waugh and Dornford Yates (234)
Raphael's *Deposition* (246)
Bernini's *Apollo and Daphne* (246)
Elaine Pagels's *The Gnostic Gospels* (248)
Irving Weinman (277)
Judith Kazantzis (277)
Evelyn Keller (278)
Gertrude Stein (281)
The Golden Ass (286)
In the Chinks of the World Machine (291)
Melanie Klein (308)
Bachelard's *The Poetics of Space* (308)
Paolo della Francesca's *Our Lady of the Pomegranate* (327)
Michelangelo (327)

PART C

Talking with Michèle Roberts: two interviews in 2003 and 2010

The last part of this manuscript comprises two conversations I had with Michèle Roberts, one in 2003 and the last one in 2010. Both interviews took place in London, one in her apartment and the other in a coffee shop near the British Museum. I would like to thank both, *Atlantis: Revista de la Asociación Española de Estudios Anglo-Americanos* and the *Journal of International Women's Studies,* for allowing me to reproduce both interviews in this book.

Talking about women, history and writing with Michèle Roberts

In the first conversation, Michèle Roberts talked about her last work at that time, *Reader, I Married Him* (2005). As she kept on talking, we get to know this story through the voice of a fifty-year-old woman. This interview, which took place in Roberts's apartment in London when I was working on my doctoral thesis, is about the combination of women, history and writing in Roberts's works of fiction.

I would like to start the conversation talking about 'writing' and its beginning in your career.

Um. Well, I think I was like all other children in English primary schools. You were encouraged to write little stories, poems, etc. I also kept a diary. I began keeping a diary when I was about ten. I lived in a family where people read a lot. My parents both read, so we had a lot of books at home. My English grandmother, who lived with us, was a great storyteller. So, she, I think, gave me a sense of the magic of storytelling. My father had written stories about the war, the Second World War, but had never managed to get them published, but I knew he was an unfulfilled writer. So, there was that background. Then, I think probably the fact that I grew up with two languages made me interested in language because I grew up bilingual in English and French. And I think as a child born in two cultures, this is obviously with hindsight, I needed to work out what culture I belonged in.

And when you write, I think, you can invent a culture. And, I think, a second major reason for becoming a writer was the misogyny of the culture I grew up in, particularly the Catholic culture. It made me want to fight back and talk about women and become a woman, in a way, in a fantasy, because real women, according to the Church and the culture, were these terrible beings. I hated them and I didn't want to be one. I didn't want to be a woman. So, again, I had to invent something that was bearable. And I think that did help me to become a writer.

And this figure of the grandmother that you just mentioned appears a lot in your novels, all the time. You can find her in The Book of Mrs Noah, The Visitation *and your current experience is very relevant in the books, isn't it?*

Yes, I think the figure of my grandmother was ... she is like the figure in Alice Miller, that psychoanalyst who writes about childhood. If you have been witnessed, in some way, by one loving person, then you're going to be OK. And because I had a difficult relationship with my own mother when I was young, my grandmother was somebody who I knew loved me, unconditionally. That was incredibly helpful. And she was very, very honest. And that made me trust her very much. She spoke the truth, always, even if it was very unpleasant. It didn't matter, it was the truth. She was very loving. She loved me. So, that's a wonderful combination for a child, I think. So she is a kind of muse. She really is. Yes.

All the main topics developed by feminism also take place in your novels, but you express them in connection with writing all the time.

So the protagonists in the novel usually develop, in an active way, the writing technique. Then how important is writing for these characters that show feelings of sisterhood, envy, etc. in your novels, dualities ...?

Well, obviously, they wouldn't have to be writers. And I don't ... I think I started to be interested in characters in folklore and religion, actually. And they were my saints, if you like. And that probably got to its apotheosis with Josephine and all the saints in *Impossible Saints*. And now, I think, I am writing more explicitly about writers because they are my new saints. But again, of course, very imperfect, flawed saints. But I suppose the point about being interested in characters who are writers is that, there is that quality of invention, that writing could stand as a metaphor for people who try to invent themselves and invent their lives, and invent a world they want to live in, which I think is probably quite fundamental to human beings. But many people would just do it in fantasy or in dream. Or they would do it through watching movies or playing games on the internet, or you know whatever. Because my interest is in language, I think, I choose to show people doing it through writing. It's not so much that I think writing has an elevated or elitist place. For me it's quite a practical down-to-earth thing. But it's also a way of playing, yes.

So if you are writing about someone writing, you are showing that even as a grown-up person, they can play, rearrange the world. And I think that's fun.

Yes that's fun, good. Would you say that your writing style is part of postmodernism and poststructuralism in the sense that you use intertextuality, and I would say, the pastiche technique where you take parts of different stories and you mix them together and create like a work?

Well, I think I began as a modernist. I think my first novel certainly was modernist in that its experimenting form was to follow the zigzag and the spiral of memory. And to attack a traditional, well it tried to attack a traditional form of storytelling which had, I think, entrapped and bruised women. So, it tried to do something very, very different. And I think I became aware of living in a postmodernist age, as I got older. And decided yes, this is a useful way of looking at how to write, how to read. Yes, I'll let myself experiment with this. I don't know what I am now because I'm probably still postmodernist in that collage goes on interesting me, *pastiche* goes on interesting me. I hope that it's more than just something decorative. I think *pastiche* for me is very, potentially subversive. When I wrote what I call my homage to romantic novels, *Fair Exchange*, I very deliberately was using a kind of romance form but very deliberately writing about eighteenth century revolutionary feminists, so wanting to subvert form again, not just imitate it. I think subversion for me is an important tenet of personal movement. I don't like the acquiescent nature of personal living, the way that everything is equal to everything else. Nothing has any real meaning.

That isn't a side of postmodernism I enjoy. I am an old Lefty, I'm a feminist. I can't think like that but I'll use postmodernism for my own end. But I think that's how a writer operates. You may be possessed by the unconscious and possessed by language, but you're not just a conduit for things to flow through. I mean you try to interact with history; you try to interact with form, so you interact with postmodernism.

You've also mentioned before that some of these protagonists in your novels use the unconscious world all the time. And some of your novels start with a death or darkness straight away. Is this unconscious a kind of free state for them to start writing and being themselves?

Yes, I think so. That's a very nice way of putting it. I noticed in mid-career that I nearly always began with a death which I hadn't realised I did. Although *The Visitation* interestingly opens with a birth but it's then immediately a death, of course. The moment they are born, they are done for. So, yes, I write about the unconscious as a place and I also think I write about the unconscious as a kind of energy and a kind of language formation.

It's a kind of poetic language. And it is a free space, particularly for these women because I think women have been so repressed into the unconscious of the culture if you like, that (a) it's where we've belonged but (b) it's where we can begin to invent ourselves. And I think there I have been encouraged by those French philosophers like Kristeva and Cixous and Irigaray who I think suggested to me in the seventies and early eighties that because so many meanings of woman were repressed, it was very liberating for a writer to dive down, and see what she can find, and bring it back up to the surface. And I go on feeling very inspired by the unconscious. And it's not quite death as a place of liberation, but perhaps death signifies the unconscious, or what's underneath. But I think there is another sense in which the reason I've always started with a dead body is that, it's about anger, perhaps. It's about a maternal body that's dead or absent or lost, and, perhaps, a child fantasising she's killed her mother through being very angry with her. And then the process of making the novel is a process of resurrection. And life happens at the end. The novels nearly always end like real life, about finding words. They nearly always end on an image of finding language. So the dead body in the beginning sits up and can speak at the end. So that's like a Freudian version, I suppose, or a Kleinian version of what I'm doing. And I would like to stress that this just happened. It wasn't that I read the theory, and thought oh, yes, I must do that. It's that I was very interested to find that the theory described what I was doing. I mean, it probably made me feel very supportive actually.

Religion, and especially Catholicism, is another very relevant topic in your novels and it has been part of your upbringing and education. I can see a positive message through your work in relation to women. You criticise historical religion, but at the same time, there is a message of freedom, change and liberation especially in the way characters like Mary Magdalene in The Wild Girl *or Mrs Noah in* The Book of Mrs Noah *express themselves. Do you intend to show in your novels how religion has conditioned the division between men and women? I mean, history has been very relevant in our position as women, but religion has been like the main institution, shall we say. Then again through your novels, I would say that you try to make these women, as you said before, not eternal but alive through the words.*

Yes, you see I think the Church has been an institution of great oppression to women. Of course, to men too. I really don't think the Church gave much to women at all. But since we have had the Church for centuries and the history of being a human being, of woman in this case, was connected to the history of the Church, that's what we have to battle. So, I think my attitude is that I'm telling stories about women who fight back, who might be crushed by the Church in some ways, but might find ways, even through the Church, to fight back. But it's not that the Church liberates women. The Church, I think, is misogynistic and oppressive and terrible. The Catholic Church is a force of dreadfulness in history, but women are very clever. They fight back. They become heretics. They involve themselves in alternative religions. They become poets. There is a long tradition of mystical writing by women: poetry and prose which resists the Church and proposes alternatives.

Fantastic and powerful stuff. You know, Teresa of Ávila was questioned by the Inquisition because she was a Jewish mystic operating within the Church. It's a very exciting story. So, I think one of the things women say as mystics and heretics and rebels and saints is that the division between men and women is false, in the interest of institutions, and of course one of the divisions between men that most hurts more women is that we are given the body and men are given the spirit, the intellect, and therefore, the power of authority. And that's a very damaging split between men and women. And I think what interests me about the real historical writings of women that you can see through the centuries, who are often nuns because that's how you got an education, is that there is an attempt, I think, to challenge the split, to explore the conflict it brings up for us as women and to propose alternative ways of being. Now, this was often, of course, couched in mystical terms, in terms of union with Christ as the beloved. So, it's not as though it's an explicitly feminist message. It couldn't be. But it does interest me that there's a reclaiming of the body as good, so that union with God can be felt and expressed in bodily terms. There is a claiming of Jesus as a mother, and he has breasts and feeds us or he has a belly in which we hide because he is pregnant with us. So, I'm enchanted by the way that rebellion against the Church can be expressed through religious terminology. And of course, the Church then comes and stamps a foot and says you must not do this, it's wrong. It's out of order.

I think some male mystics did it too but they reclaimed the body in their mystical writing. They didn't just talk about being souls and being intimate. They acknowledged the power of divine love as a bodily force. So it's as though mystical language and poetry offered a level on which to explore a possibility of reconciling body and soul of both sexes, which makes it very subversive and very critical, I think.

What is the relationship between the protagonists in your novels and men. Do you develop the concept that Jung defended between the 'animus' and the 'anima'?

Well, I did at one point, I think. When I was writing in the early eighties, I think I was very interested in that. I think my book of Mary Magdalene *The Wild Girl* shows that. It's saturated with Jungian thought. And I don't know that I'd write it in the same way now.

I think also *The Visitation*, which is the one before, is pretty Jungian. And I think *Mrs Noah* in some respect is. I still think, although it is just perhaps I wouldn't use Jungian terms perhaps that means I've simply incorporated them into my language. I think we share a DNA. So we've got to be all somehow the same in some deep, deep sense. If we can fall in love with each other as heterosexuals, we must have a way of knowing and understanding the other. So again, there's something shared. On the other hand, I do believe that I began to think, as I've got older I suppose, that for a woman the fact of becoming pregnant and giving birth is a profound experience because men simply don't share it, although technology is catching up very quickly, so we'll see in the next fifty years, won't we? So that difference, it seems to me, could affect you in how you feel and think about what it means to be a woman. Now many women have very different views on that, and that's what interests me. We're not all going to be the same about it. But given that it's a biological difference, women can think about it and men can. This is all very cautious, because as you get older you get wilder, but you get more cautious. And I still think that history and culture affect us around gender. But I don't think I'd go so far as the queer theory people who would say that even gender is not enough just to have a playfulness about gender. We are going to have a right, right away, because of the possibilities offered by technology and, you know, by our bodies.

But also, I think, by things like the Internet. We can simply be whatever we want, whenever we want, all the time. I don't think I've gone that far, because I think for most women in the world, at the moment, you know, the nurturing of children is pretty important, and the giving of food, the finding of food. So it seems to me it's quite a luxury for people with access to higher technology to have extremes of queer theory. And I am more interested in the kind of daily message of what it is to be a woman. Although I know for your generation, people don't think about it as much as my generation. Which is wonderful. All the students that I teach, the young women think, you know, I can be whatever I want, I can write whatever I want. This is fabulous. I think it's a wonderful freedom, I salute it. I don't think you have to go around thinking about I am a woman all the time. You do whatever you want [*laughing*].

In relation to The Book of Mrs Noah, *considering Mrs Noah a silenced historical character, do you intend to rewrite a history or a 'herstory,' putting words into writing from the character's points of view? Do you think it's possible to relate historical events with fiction considering that in both cases the subjective point of view of the narrator is inevitable?*

Well, I think, I don't say 'herstory' because for me the linguistics is history and I think all of us, actually as writers can become interested in history, men as much as women. So women's history is what I might say – or men's history – you know, working class history.

I think the new history, which is now being written, makes us see that we can find the voices, for example, of working class people, of black people. If we look hard enough, there is more there than we thought, as I found with the voices of women in ancient archives. So, the new history is much more democratic, it's much richer; it's much wider, because it's drawing on a much bigger section of the population. And I think it's made us see that historical records are, to some extent, subjective. I want to believe that objective truth can be sought. But I think that at the same time, in a contradictory way, I know that it's always inflected by subjectivity, because it will reveal the interests of a particular class. So, for example, Church history will reveal the interest of priests and popes. And probably, the history written by abbesses will be subjective in another way. It's not just that male dominated history is bad and the other one is good.

This is such an enormous and complex question because I still believe, I think, in truth and lies, and yet I know that we find it very hard to tell the truth because we are subjects and we are conditioned by the unconscious, by our own past, by our fantasies, by our dreams, and by our desires. So in a sense, I think, I see the novelist as a sort of historian and as a sort of biographer, and that we have a lot in common. We're all writing narratives and I think what the form has in common, if you like, is history as a narrative, a novel as a narrative, a biography as a narrative, a saint's life as a narrative. The point about a narrative is it's after the event. A story is something you compose after the event and that's what interests me as a writer. It's the shape; it's about a shape, to put a shape on things. It's a very long-winded answer [*laughing*].

In relation to Gaffer, *I'm going to compare* Gaffer *with Adam in* The Mistressclass *because I could see that in both stories you've got writers, and it seems that Gaffer and Adam are just blocked. They're not able to write. However, both Vinny and Catherine in* The Mistressclass, *or the sibyls and Mrs Noah, can write without stopping. Do you try again to use parody and just reverse the history of writing?*

Yes, a bit, but I thought the sibyls all started off with writers' block. I thought that's why they came on the ark, they have all got writers' block. So it isn't just that they can write without stopping and the men can't. I don't think I'm doing that. It isn't a simple reversal.

I was interested in the sources of writers' block, whether it's gendered in any way. And I think for women writers, it can be. But there's a joke about God, yes, having written one bestseller, what do you do next? I just felt, yes, he could do with a bit of a reversal, like turning upside down. You see in *The Mistressclass*, I think I'm trying to say something about good writing and bad writing. And for me, Catherine is a bad writer. She is somebody who's sold her soul. She's writing what I consider a series of lies or bad fantasies because I don't go along with the postmodern idea that any old erotica is wonderful. For me, Catherine is writing, she is writing about women wanting to be heard and wanting to be punished as a sort of pay-off, having some power in the world. So, I was amazed when all the reviewers said 'Oh yes, she's writing erotica.' I deliberately said she's writing sadomasochism. And it's not that I don't want to explore that or I don't think it's interesting, but she is writing about it in a kind of cheap, exploitative way. Whereas Vinny, I think, is a purer writer because she is willing to be poor in order to pursue her vision.

Adam is simply blocked for very personal reasons; he hasn't dealt with his feelings about this father. And I suppose that something I feel about a lot of men is that masculinity has become a subject for them. If they face it, they would write very interesting things. But if they block it off, maybe they would get stuck. So I was seeing it with Adam in quite a personal and subjective way. It's just he's had a really rough time with this very difficult father. I don't think I was being kind of political about male writers in this respect. And, of course, the problem with poor old Charlotte Brontë, the ghost of Charlotte Brontë, is that she's writing away for dear life, but she's burning her letters. So, it's a kind of terrible writing, really. That's masochistic, I think. She's writing for somebody else, not really for herself. And then she's giving it away and she's burning it. And of course, she doesn't exist anyway because she's dead and it's a ghost talking. So, I think I'm more ambivalent, actually, about the women writers than you are admitting [*both laughing*].

I'll just add something else. I was very tender in my mind towards Adam because it's the first time that I've written at length from inside a male character. And I got very fond of him. And that was a nice discovery. I mean, OK, he's having problems, he looks weak. But I was very intrigued by him. I enjoyed creating a man. So that was a nice breakthrough for me.

I'm just going to go now to The Mistressclass. *I've just got a couple of questions in relation to that. And I have read, in relation to* The Mistressclass, *because you're using Charlotte Brontë, that you are more identified with writers from the nineteenth century like Charlotte Brontë than contemporary writers like Angela Carter or Fay Weldon, for example. How much of this influence appears in* The Mistressclass *or in the whole of your novels?*

Well, first of all, there is a difference between saying 'I like writing about writers of the nineteenth century,' simply because they are a hundred and fifty years ago and there's a certain licence in freedom. That doesn't mean I'm not inspired by some twentieth century writers. I really am. You know, Toni Morrisson has been a major influence on me. Angela Carter has been an influence, but I think more in her fairy stories, *The Bloody Chamber*, than her novels. Fay Weldon is not an inspiration, that's quite true. But it's not that I'm not interested in contemporary writers. I read them, voraciously, all the time. So, whoever said that was wrong. Sorry, tell me the second bit of the question?

I was asking you how much of this influence of the nineteenth century writers appears in your novels.

Well, you see, what happens is that you fall in love and you don't consciously choose who to fall in love with. But when you fall in love in real life, the person gets kind of lit up and they sort of shine golden, and of course it's because you're projecting to them. You know, it's your own light that projects, but you don't realise it, you think there's that amazing person. So I'd had an experience with falling in love that got me interested through a very circular route with George Sand, actually. But I didn't quite feel that I could write about her directly, partly because, I think, she wrote so much about herself that she's very known. Somehow my beam of light switched aside to Charlotte Brontë when I fell in love with her. I've always been in love with Charlotte Brontë, actually, ever since I was about ten. But I suddenly felt I can write about her now. But I think it's because she was hopelessly in love with the teacher. And again, it's this writing thing about what does it mean to have a mentor who is a man, a mentor who is a teacher, a mentor who tells you that you write in over elaborate and baroque ways. A mentor who is married. It brings up all kinds of very interesting issues. Perhaps, particularly because in Britain there's been a real issue in universities about sexual harassment. What does it mean to be a young woman student with a charismatic male teacher? Do you feel free and liberated? Or do you feel that there is too much sex coming from them? I mean, these are all very important questions, I think, for young women students and of course, they also fall in love with their teachers. We all know this. So, I wanted to write about that as a subject. But I think if you write about something like that very directly, it can come across like journalism. And I hate that kind of novel where it's like a journalist in disguise, I hate it. What I learnt from Charlotte Brontë is, as a writer, you can use metaphor, and she learnt that from Shakespeare. So you can structure your novel like a Shakespearean play with a subtext of metaphor. You can also actually put Charlotte Brontë in it, which is what I wanted to do.

Obviously, I couldn't yet write a novel about Angela Carter. She is too recently dead. She's too alive for me in that sense. But I was very inspired by her and by Calvino and, you know, by all the writers of my generation, Casanses, A. S. Byatt was doing it, I was doing it, retelling old stories with that personal link on. And of course, Carter does it really beautifully in *The Bloody Chamber*. I mean, her language is very rich and very voluptuous. Marina Warner also.

So, I think I've been getting permission from all those writers to write in a voluptuous and imagistic way. And that was very helpful for me as a writer. And one day, maybe, I'll write more about George Sand because she continues to fascinate me. As indeed when I fell in love with Flaubert and Mallarmé, I put them into *The Looking Glass*. I made a composite male writer out of them because I had fallen in love with them. They had lit up and begun to glow.

Is Doris Lessing another writer that you admire?

Yes and no. I admired her enormously in the seventies, but then I became irritated by her omniscient narrators. They seem to me too lofty and potentially scornful of ordinary humanity. So, I don't really admire her any more as a writer. I feel bad saying that because you know, she is a great writer. But I had to have a big fight with her. She is like a mother figure woman, so I had to have a big fight with her to break loose and write differently. I don't believe in omniscient narrators. If I put them in, it's for a very, very difficult reason.

Yes, usually you use the first person narrator all the time.

Or I use the third person, you know, that Flaubertian thing, just looking over the shoulder. That kind of omniscient one, I'm going to fight it because it's God the father, for me. It's an authority figure.

Would you say that Vinny in The Mistressclass *and Charlotte Brontë have some kind of similarity as the two of them can be writers who are in love with a married person and are, in a way, independent. Will you agree with this?*

Yes, I think what I was doing was to some extent taking the Charlotte Brontë story and saying 'what if' it happened again in the present. So Vinny does in a sense represent Charlotte, but she also has bits of Emily, I think so. But the fact that I've got two pairs of sisters. Yes, it's a replay.

And madness is again another topic that appears in the novel if we consider Madame Heger's madness as it becomes visible in Jane Eyre's *character. The same happens again in* The Mistressclass *because at some point, I saw Adam mad at the end of the novel. Again you're just swapping, according to my point of view, the roles. It's Adam the one that becomes mad because he cannot really see.*

That's very interesting. I didn't see that. What I thought was, really I was exploring in Charlotte's letters, in her impossible letters what it is to be mad when madness means possession, obsession, stalking, mad love, mad desire. If there are no boundaries, that's probably a kind of madness. But of course, Charlotte contains it because she contains it through literary form in letters. So it's actually quite safe. I think for Adam, it wasn't that I was reversing. But I was saying something about a man that can be extremely vulnerable and can lose touch with something called reality. So in that jumping off the bridge, falling off, it is a plunging to the waters of the unconscious. But it's more; you could also see it as a plunging to the unconscious which is a good thing. You could see it as a rite of passage. You could see it as a baptism, a journey of discovery, because madness, of course can be all those things. So it's not a simple opposition of madness and sanity. I've always been interested in madness because I think it's not clear-cut. I know it's easy to romanticise it.

People who are mad can suffer enormously. I know that. But I think that if you're helped to understand what is going on, then madness can be a bridge into a better, richer life. I think that's true, because it's usually about the unconscious coming up. Then if you are helped to cope with it, then you get somewhere better. And I think for Adam that is what I thought happened. So madness is a shorthand, isn't it? And he's more interesting than Catherine. Catherine is totally depressed. She's half dead. She's an awful person. I really didn't like her.

Just to conclude, would you say that your novels make a revision and a rewriting of the metanarratives that we have – history and religion – that have controlled our thoughts, our behaviour and our conditions. And are you trying to contribute to make those voices from the past be heard and expressed with freedom in your novels? Are you at the same time joining all times and all women in your fiction throughout the short stories?

Gosh! That's three cosmic questions in one [*laughing*]. I think I am trying to challenge the metanarratives. Yes, and I do that through working with form as well as content, so that the kinds of narratives or stories I'm making simply are part of the critique, which is expressing the content. And I know that sounds very pompous.

That's your other question about joining all women across history because I do actually, as a Marxist, you know, I was trained. I went to university and did a lovely literature degree on Medieval Language and Literature and I had a fantastic time. I got out of university and began to educate myself as a thinker, which I hadn't been before. And I joined the Marxist study group and I became a Lefty and I read Freud. So I have a concept of history, but it's quite a Marxist one. History really matters. On the other hand, as a woman with an imagination, who is a writer, you kind of fly through history. And, you know that definition that it's like I've got my knees apart with bits of skirt, so they're separate, but you can just do that and they meet. And that's what you are doing as a novelist very often. It's different ways of thinking. And the unconscious. You know, I dream at night and I'm talking to dead people, I talk to my grandmother. You know, what is going on? So, the two things co-exist. On the one hand, recognising the specificity of history, on the other hand, cherishing what the imagination can do. But I don't believe in, a historical, 'all women are together everywhere for ever more.' Because actually that's almost like an imperialism, actually, as a way of thinking. And I think as a Lefty, I'm more and more aware of that, but as a white woman, I can speak for my experience and my imagination. But I cannot speak for anyone in the world in a simple way. That would be to colonise it. On the other hand, if I wanted to write about black women in Africa, I could have a go, but I would have to go and do a lot of research. I can't just rely on imagination. So, it's incredibly complicated and I've given you a very simplistic reply. I'm struggling with that a lot at the moment, partly because of teaching and talking to the young people in my classes. We talk a lot about this issue because we have a very multicultural group of students. We disagree, we all disagree about how free are we as writers to write about whatever we want. And we all say that we are. And yet we can have quarrels when it comes to how we do it. Is it accurate? Is it authentic? What do those words mean? It's very interesting, actually. For example, I mean, there is a story that I rather like in *Flesh and Blood* which was inspired by seventeenth century Italian culture.

I did a lot of research for that story, I wanted to get the details right, so that then, my imagination can take off and I suppose that's how I see it, that history really matters. You look at an authentic church record written by a real scribe in the seventeenth century. The real handwriting, the real document, the events, so far as we know real, copied, written down, his version, his glosses, his mistakes. All of that is a reality. But then, as a writer I'll fly off. And I feel able to do that. I feel licensed, which is perhaps a very bourgeois notion of writerly freedom, I'm sure it is. But I think I'm more and more sort of coming to terms with that, thinking, OK, I'm confined by my history, my feminism is a white woman's history. I'm from a middle class family. My father was working class, didn't have any education, got me an education. I became middle class. My mother's family is middleclass. I'm white. I can try and criticise myself, I can try and understand my formation, I can try and change, I can try and struggle with myself, but I also cherish what made me.

I cherish even the old bloody Catholic Church. Because it gave me language, it gave me stories, it gave me folklore. So it's a mixture of self-criticism, self-knowledge, and a kind of jumping up with the imagination.

Thank you very much for your conversation.

Thank you for your good questions and for making me think [*both laughing*].

Works Cited

Brontë, Charlotte. *Jane Eyre*. London: Penguin, 1847. Print.
Carter, Angela. *The Bloody Chamber*. London: Penguin, 1981. Print.
Jung, Carl G., and R. Wilhelm. *El secreto de la Flor de Oro*. Barcelona: Paidós, 1996. Print.
Liseux, Thérese of. *Story of a Soul: The Autobiography of St. Thérese of Liseux*. Institute of Carmelite St.: ICS Publications, 1996. Print.

A conversation with Michèle Roberts about novels, history and autobiography

In the following interview, Michèle Roberts talked about her novels and especially about her memoir. She described how her autobiographical account, *Paper Houses: A Memoir of the '70s and Beyond* (2007) took place mainly in the city of London during revolutionary years for young women who wanted to be heard and who wanted to be part of the public domain. Michèle Roberts also talked about her beginnings as a writer during the 1970s in the capital of England. The figure of the female *flâneur,* who strolls around London to explore and to observe instead of being observed, was also discussed in this conversation.

This last discussion took place in a café during my research stay at the Institute of English Studies (IES), School of Advanced Studies at the University of London on 13th August 2010. I would like to thank both the IES at the University of London for their hospitality and support while I visited them, and the Agencia Canaria the Investigación, Innovación y Sociedad de la Información (ACIISI), for funding this research stay. Without the support of both institutions this conversation may have not taken place. My special thanks to Michèle Roberts for sharing some of her time to discuss her work with me.

Hi Michèle, thank you very much for your time here today.
Hi.
The first question I would like to ask you is, obviously, I have enjoyed thoroughly the reading and analysis of Paper Houses: A Memoir of the '70s and Beyond. *And I cannot stop connecting your memoir with those autobiographical writings by Virginia Woolf. Why have you chosen the form of the memoir to write one of your most recent literary works? Have you preserved that polarity between fiction and fact or between the narrator and the character?*

I have to tell you something quite banal which is that my dear publisher suggested that I write a memoir. It was her idea. I then thought what I should write about. And I thought. I'd like to write about the seventies because I think they've become very misrepresented in modern culture at the time of cultural self-indulgent, nonsense, on the one hand, and the glamour of Baroque, but also, on the other hand, puritanical feminisms. And of course, feminism wasn't puritanical. So I thought I can set the record straight. And I also realised in the seventies when I did get going as a writer, so it was about my beginnings. And because I am a kind of Marxist too I've believed in history and that memory involves history in complicated ways. I was going to write about myself starting as a writer and about the seventies and I had to write about the politics of the time which I was very involved in as a woman and as a writer.

So, for the second part of your question, I quickly realised that to write a memoir, you have to give it a form, a shape. And that's where you draw upon your fictional knowledge of the form. Because similar chronology isn't enough, I think. Well to get it published these days, there has to be a story. So, I came up with this idea of a story about my move from house to house, to house to house. And it would be a story not only about what happens in the house but about the haunting on the street because that is where politics will happen, on the street, for women just as much as for men. Because the whole thing about the women movement was about women. We could leave our house and could live beyond the street and demonstrate, make theatre, enjoy ourselves, go for walks, meet each other. So that is how the form of the memoir slowly arrived.

In relation to Virginia Woolf, would you say that she was a kind of literary mother in your writing?

Well, she is and she isn't and that is perhaps what you'd say about all mothers, that you are ambivalent about them. You love them and hate them. They give you life but also they smack you in the face. So, of course she was a major influence on me as a young woman reader. And I think I admire the way in which every sentence is so downfall, created. She is never banal. On the other hand, I thought because her novels had really very little about the body in them, not really a visible, sweaty, bloody, shitting body. But I did find it very interesting. In her diaries there is much more body. And in her letters. So when she is at *The Lighthouse* (1927), for example, the body is there. And then one of her memoirs, which is really beautiful, *Moments of Being* (1976), that I think I read several times. And she starts really with a bodily life of the child that she was. And I think somehow she is connecting that to the desire to write. She does it much more open. This is at the end of her life. So the child's and young woman's bodily lives are connected to writing, whereas in her novels, that connection is very implicit.

Also, Michèle you don't mind that I use your first name, of course... You have become a prolific writer dedicated to different written forms but you have mostly written novels. What correspondence do you see between the woman's novel and the woman's memoir?

First of all, I would just need to say that although my publishers were thought postmodern, they are very close to modern poetry. And they have quite other connections with other forms like theatre or plays. I think I became interested in fictional forms which involved looking at the inner life of the person. I am really, really interested in the secret unconscious mind and the paranoia. It may be speaking under the first person or it may be speaking over the shoulder. That does connect with the memoir, I think, because in a memoir there is a certain speaker who currently, just currently, is trying to tell the truth. And what interests me is that in a memoir apparently you can tell the truth but you can lie as much as you like, you can leave out parts as much as you like, which is really a fictional way of writing. And in a novel you are very deliberately playing that notion of telling the truth. So, for me, yes, there are bridges. And I think my work, my novels often look at the memoir. For example, *The Looking Glass* is a novel absolutely compared to the memoir in the first person. And I think, *Impossible Saints*, although it was written in the third person, it's absolutely concerned with a non-fictional form. So, for me, they interconnect but I couldn't tell you so in an abstract, theoretical way. All I can tell you is, in this particular book, I was exploring and the interconnection overlapped. So they do interconnect. And maybe one of connections is that women are traditionally told to lie, and that's quite interesting. What do you lie about? Do we lie? Shall we tell the truth? It's this Freudian thought.

Yes, another question related to your memoir and to London. London has been the location chosen to write this personal account of your life in the controversial 1970s and 1980s. Did you want to connect your own persona's progress and your identity with the urban city of London?

157

Yes, I did very much. That was half-side of me though, because I am half-French and half-English. Although I grew up in a suburb, which is half way between the country and the city, I tend to line up my father and my English life and the city. My mother was from the French countryside. And I am currently living in both the French countryside and the city of London. So, I think my formation as a young woman is really, really about the city. It's all very important to say that the city is the place where I became politicised and became a feminist.

Oh God, it's a huge topic, isn't it? Since modernism, I think, lot of radical artists were marching away from the countryside in their visions, from a world of agriculture and the reaction of all types of notions. And I think the idea of 'you cannot make art about the countryside, it has to be urban'; well, I'm not actually sure about that because I've written a novel set in the French countryside (*Daughters of the House*, for instance), which is about politics, and not about the city. When I came to write about my formation, it was about the city. Yes. That was something to do with walking the streets and meeting people. Because in the countryside you've got to walk and you don't know who you will find in your walk.

Yes, I think I do remember one example in your memoir in which you compare the city of Oxford and the city of London. And also in that comparison I remember that you criticised the male society watching you, the woman, and how scared you could feel in the countryside of Oxford and how more secured you could feel in the city of London.

True, although in the city you got harassed by men all the time, you could run away quickly round the corner, or into a shop or into a pub whereas in the countryside if you are in a field and there is a man harassing you, it's hard to get away. I mean I was harassed all the time, which is what happened to young women all the time in those days. I think women still get harassed a huge amount. Because I am older, I don't feel it in the same way. The city in that sense is a lot of safer. And the city traditionally tells us as women not to stay safe but to feel always scared.

And I wonder now, talking about cities, how much of truth was there in the story of Bangkok. Did it really happen to you?

Oh yes. It was very scary. *Thanks God that you are here.* Although this young man, I think he was also so frightened about what he had done. I mean, I did know that he wasn't going to rape me but still it was all very, very frightening.

The next question is about the female flâneur. Would you say that you have combined both modern and postmodern techniques in the writing of your personal account?

Oh God, that's a difficult question. *Both laughing.* Well I suppose, I have become aware that at the moment a lot of men are writing about walking in the city: Ian Sinclair, Peter Ackroyd. Some write about psycho geography, and sometimes of course about being a *flâneur*. And I got terribly irritated because they never refer to women, as beings that can walk around. The women are completely absent in these accounts. And I know from my reading that modernist women writers loved walking the city. They were doing it. Virginia Woolf, you know, and her diaries are full of her walking. Dorothy L. Sayers, Katherine Mansfield. I mean all these modernist women who were living and writing in London walked around the city at a time of great recording and brilliant example. And my taste of this, as a postmodernist perhaps, is to make judge. And I just noticed the word; the man is a *flâneur* and a woman who would walk the streets, a streetwalker, will be a prostitute. And I think that tradition is there. There is something deeply difficult and problematic for the woman who likes roaming the streets by her, she is still seen as a problem. And I wish all these dangerous things didn't do that. All she's, she is just harassed and aggressed. But for men is just different. It goes back to Baudelaire, the *flâneur,* doesn't it? I mean, I don't think he would walk the streets with a female companion. He was looking at women. But perhaps there is a switch for a woman to be an object and become a subject. I don't know if that is modernist or postmodernist but it makes sense. You're perceived to be the object instead of the public subject. But of course to do that you have to defy yourself a bit and respond to it. And I put the picture in here (*Paper Houses: A Memoir of the '70s and Beyond*). That is a picture of me in my outfit walking in the street. It's a self-portrait. *Oh, yes, how beautiful. I didn't know that.* Yes. *Both laughing.*

Let's keep talking about women's writing. In Paper Houses, *as in most of your works of fiction, you have used the first person narration to tell the personal story, which, at the same time, is connected to the public history. Could you talk a little bit about that connection between the inner and the outer worlds in* Paper Houses *as part of your developing identity, or as part of a rebirth?*

Gosh. It was a kind of project to try to map the inner life to the outer life and remap that outer life back to the inner life. And I think I was doing that while I was reading about a wonderful psychoanalyst and writer called Marion Milner. She was nothing but an analyst. She wrote *On not Being Able to Paint* (1950), *Eternity's Sunrise: A Way of Keeping a Diary* (2010) and *A Life of One's Own* (1934). And she talked about creativity a great deal. And she was the first person I was reading in my late twenties who was suggesting that your inner world connected intimately to the outer world via emotions, for example, desire or fear. And I got on reading a whole project of writers. Julia Kristeva became very important. This is complicated. She talked about the way you abstract words to make your emotions. Then you might say: I felt angry or I felt great. She had this wonderful life as part of this currently bodily feeling, which we call emotions. And I connected that to the metaphor and how we make metaphor out of this currently bodily feeling. And we make the metaphor by subjecting it onto an image in the outside world which connects everything to Marion Milner's idea. And I began to see that metaphor remains profoundly important to me because it connects us to the world. It's always taking our inner life and saying: 'It's part of the universe, it's part of the world'. Because I might say: 'I'm feeling as cold as that and then I am immediately hot'. And it matters to me more and more because in the modern world metaphor is not fashionable and people are supposed to be like little atoms although we are all sort of connected by machine, mobile phone or email. With this connection, I am part of universe, which is expressed by metaphor. I'm very fond of it. I think it's incredibly important. It is a kind of religion. There is a very long way to answer it.

Yes, thank you.

Sorry, can I say something about ... Not all my novels are written in the first person. Quite a few are in the third person. *Yes, you said that* Impossible Saints *is one of them.* And it is an experiment. I come back to the first person because I feel it's always not me, that in the first person. It's a paradox. While in the third person I can be in there much.

Would you confirm that you have been concerned with the dearth of women in the critical canon of great writers by remembering and rescuing women and giving them a voice in your novels?

Yes. It's not even just in the canon of literature. It's a kind of women giving to the world. It's not recognised. It's not valued. The women are valued as mothers. They are also sentimentalised and Christianised. They may be valued as writers or scientists. But then their body would be taken away. I think culturally women are devalued when women are in the world not on the world. Because my place is writing, I look at women writers. So, yes, I would confirm it. Yes.

Just another question in relation to Paper Houses *again. You have dealt with different topics such as language, freedom, writing, sex, love, friendship, family, exploring, and marriage, among others. Marriage has always been a recurrent topic in women's narrative and in* Paper Houses *you describe two different marriages in your life, being the one with Jim the most celebrated experience in which you felt not only a woman but also an artist. Could you talk about that link between domestic life and professional writing?*

Well, I have to be very personal. That's fine. The lovely thing about Jim was that he immediately recognised me as a fellow artist. It was normal. That was wonderful. He was the first man in my life who ever thought that it was completely normal that I had become an artist. And of course, he understood feminism. He had many artist friends, many women. He liked women very much. And then he immediately offered me a home because I was homeless. And because he worked at home, we were both living in an artist studio, really. So, he didn't break the artist practice with being a father who was there at home looking after his sons. And that was really inspiring because I had quite a lot of space in the house, a space to start with my writing and together, I think, we tried to find a way where we integrated domestic life and art. And of course it was a time in which many writers were looking at those connections, anyway. I mean *post-feminists* and *post-domestic*, I think it's called. It became a subject. You know, you had Mary Kelly showing dirty nappies in the art gallery. You had women artists actually talking about housework. It was a good time. So, all I can say is integration in somehow was something that was dead but it was possible to kind of revalue domestic as a space in which things happened. Of course as a woman, I knew domestic violence happened in a domestic space; child abuse had already happened in a domestic place, rage happened in a domestic space. We tried to be living in a domestic space and also in an artistic studio. It was all very inspiring.

I don't really have a last question but I was now wondering about that domestic place, that place of your own to be writing. And I wonder if you wouldn't mind describing how it is like. How is that place of your own like when writing? Well, do you mean, in abstract or in reality? *I mean in abstract, as a writer.*

Yes, because of the idea of *Paper Houses*, it could be anywhere. That is about my life. I've lived in many places. I've moved a great deal. So, it's something temporary. It needs to have a lot of capacity for solitude view and privacy. But then it needs to be a magic place that can attract all the selves, somewhere where at 6.00 o'clock people come in, and we cook, and eat, and dance, make love, eat, get bored and drink. That's what I've conveyed in the sacred convent in *Impossible Saints* because in a way, we have to live in a guttural culture with small houses. You've seen it in Twickenham: streets and streets and streets of tiny houses. And they all have a sitting room, a kitchen, a dining room, two bedrooms for the children, one bedroom for their parents. Who gets any privacy? How can you be artist in that surrounding? In England men go to their shed. To the garden shed is where the man goes and the woman has nowhere to go. So, I talk about this all the time with my partner as half of the time we live together, and half of the time I say no, it's impossible. I wouldn't have much space because he is a psychiatrist and works at home. So, this ideal place really has a table, a chair, and I'll have a laptop, and I think it'll have a window. Ideally, it has a little garden. So, it is a paper house folded up. It's a book. It really is. And then, yes, I am very materialistic. You know in my fantasies, I'd love to live in a very beautiful house, very luxurious, a French manor house, blablabla. I don't have the money for that. I've always lived in small places but I'm very happy. So, really my house, my writing house really is my imagination. It really, really is. The time and space here is also a paper house. As soon as I have a view, I could sit here with my diary, my notebook and this is a house because at the time we are talking we have made a house. I really believe it's true.

OK, thank you very much for your time here today, Michèle. That was very interesting.

Well, thank you!

Both Laughing

Works Cited

Milner, Marion. *A Life of One's Own*. London: Routledge, 2010. Print.
---. *Eternity's Sunrise: A Way of Keeping a Diary*. London: Routledge, 2010. Print.
---. *On not Being Able to Paint*. London: Routledge, 2010. Print.
Roberts, Michèle. *A Piece of the Night*. London: The Women's Press, 1978. Print.
---. *The Visitation*. London: The Women's Press, 1983. Print.
---. *The Wild Girl*. London: Minerva, 1984. Print.
---. *The Book of Mrs Noah*. London: Vintage, 1987. Print.
---. *In the Red Kitchen*. London: Vintage, 1990. Print.
---. *Daughters of the House*. London: Virago Press, 1992. Print.
---. *Flesh and Blood*. London: Virago Press, 1994. Print.
---. *Impossible Saints*. London: Virago Press, 1997. Print.
---. *Food, Sex & God: On Inspiration and Writing*. London: Virago Press, 1998. Print.
---. *Fair Exchange*. London: Little Brown, 1999. Print.

---. *The Looking Glass*. London: Little Brown, 2000. Print.
---. *The Mistressclass*. London: Little Brown, 2003. Print.
---. *Paper Houses: A Memoir of the '70s and Beyond*. London: Virago Press, 2007. Print.
Woolf, Virginia. *To the Lighthouse*. Boston: Mariner Books, 1989. Print.
---. *Moments of Being*. Ed. Jeanne Schulkind. New York: Harcourt Brace & Company, 1985. Print.

Conclusions

> Three further associated factors which have emerged over this period have been the growth of women's economic activity, a dramatic rise in male economic inactivity rates and the transition of London from being a mono-ethnic to becoming a multi-ethnic city. These changes further set these non-middle-class groups apart from a working class that was historically white, male and employed in manual occupations. (Butler and Hamnett 225)

Although I have tried to present this book with a researcher's voice, I have also intended to write this manuscript with a form that is shared by other women's writing, a form that combines the inside with the outside, the personal with the political. Life is change and constant evolution. History is memory, understanding and reflection. As suggested in this quote, women have gained financial independence in London. With her literary work, Michèle Roberts has aimed to see that women's emancipation needs to look into public history and also into private life in order to keep moving forward.

Travelling in Women's History with Michèle Roberts: Literature, Language and Culture has combined facts and awareness with regard to Michèle Roberts's literary work. I have intended to analyse Roberts's novels and memoir by having in mind both history and fiction. The combination of reality and imagination has awakened thoughts and perceptions in my mind. Roberts's novels and memoir have inspired me through theory, not the other way around. It is from the private side that the public arena is being achieved. As a woman scholar I have meant to portray this feminist consciousness in this book.

It has been my purpose to illustrate that Michèle Roberts rewrites stories of known events or personalities in order to allow her heroines to express their own bodies. This contemporary novelist has explored different modern and postmodern techniques in her writing style. Michèle Roberts allows some of her heroines to communicate in the first person narrative as it happened with *The Wild Girl, The Looking*

Glass or *The Mistressclass*, for instance. Roberts's heroines have been inspired by historical and religious personalities like Mary Magdalene, Saint Teresa of Ávila, Mary Wollstonecraft, and Charlotte Brontë, among others. They have been rescued to convey with their own language what their bodies are.

By means of the novel, Roberts contributes to the feminist movement because she uses her fiction to criticise the marginalised condition women have had to face in history and religion. Literature allows space for imagination while history tries to be true to reality. With the writing of novels, Roberts offers the possibility of rewriting stories in which the main characters are rescued from being good or bad, passive or active, virgin or whore. Instead, Roberts's protagonists need darkness and the unconscious in order that they can feel liberated and express themselves as they really are. Roberts's heroines often find their emancipation by means of writing their selves and by combining opposites. Roberts has questioned gender issues in her narrative. She agrees with Virginia Woolf when she declares that 'writing's a bisexual practice: you have to be both active and passive; masculine and feminine need to be in relation' (Roe et all 172-73).

The personal and public backgrounds have been considered in the analysis of Michèle Roberts's work. The combination of the French and the English cultures together with the Protestant and Catholic religions have shaped most of Roberts's novels in which references to her inner and outer sides are repeatedly manifested. Michèle Roberts's heroines have been inspired by historical and mystical women who become everyday protagonists in her narrations looking for a language that corresponds to their bodies. Roberts has dealt with a variety of topics such as feminism, women's history, sexuality, storytelling, writing as woman, body and language, Catholicism, darkness and motherhood, to name a few.

Paper Houses: A Memoir of the '70s and Beyond has been the text dedicated to the second part of this analysis. *Paper Houses* is a fictional and historical memoir of a contemporary, feminist writer who walks about London city as a woman *flâneur* to deal with social, political and personal issues from both modern and postmodern perspectives. Michèle Roberts has revisited her own past in order to write a personal account of her life dealing with not always trustworthy memory, her past diaries and her personal experiences. Michèle Roberts has also highlighted body and language, personal and political as binaries that are present in her narrative. Moreover, with *Paper Houses* the author has revisited her inner thoughts and rediscovered her identity and her true devotion to become a professional writer whatever difficult and poor circumstances she had to face. The protagonist had to move to different communal houses where she separated from her family and where she managed to share language and conversations with friends. *Paper Houses* is about killing the angel in the house and about surviving the implications this battle requires. *Paper Houses* is also that room of her own, that room that allows creativity and the writing of the self, that room where the writer finally belongs. *Paper Houses* is the mental place for writing and creation. With *Paper Houses*, Roberts has acknowledged that she is an activist feminist writer who considers her personal and political sides at the time of creating language and context in her novels. As an experimental writer, Roberts has gone deep inside her unconscious in order to position herself observing as a modern and liberated female *flâneur* but with non-established postmodern connotations. Roberts concludes her memoir of the 1970s and beyond by being in her house, built up by paper, where she is not an angel but a devoted writer.

Paper Houses: A Memoir of the '70s and Beyond is a text in print created by personal, cultural and historical memories, recollected diaries, photos and revisited realities and fantasies of a young and revolutionary past in London. As an autobiographical text, Roberts's memoir intertwines history with fiction, public with personal, and body with mind. The writer-protagonist links her present achievements with her revisited past.

Roberts's memoir has a dual perspective. The female *flâneur* observes as a young protagonist in her past. Likewise, she is being observed by the contemporary memoirist in order to analyse personal, cultural and political subject matters of the controversial 1970s and beyond in the capital of London. Roberts has dealt with language, words, sexuality, religion, family, friends, being lonely, being in community, being a woman and being a writer, among other topics. *Paper Houses* has also dealt not only with marriage as a domestic theme but also with earning money as a professional woman writer who has to face poverty and survive private and public spaces. The writing of this contemporary memoir is 'about asserting and revising their [the writers] versions of reality', as Helen Buss also suggested (xvii).

Paper Houses shares common characteristics with autobiographies, novels and travel writing in search for Roberts's construction as an independent woman and as a professional writer. *Paper Houses* has offered the contemporary and feminist writer a revision of her life, using her own psyche, her own memory and her own documents and knowledge. From scrawl, *Paper Houses, A Memoir of the '70s and Beyond* is a literary creation, an experimental text shared, and a story that completes some of the gaps left behind by the history of the 1970s and 1980s in London.

Travelling in Women's History with Michèle Roberts's Novels: Literature, Language and Culture is only one of many, varied journeys that can be fulfilled. At present, some women are travelling with knowledge, language, books, and private and public places in which they deal with language, society, history, religion and culture. Every day journeys of all types are taking place, physically and metaphorically and we must keep travelling. One day all women and men will accept and respect each other as equals. When that moment arrives, new journeys will need to be discovered and experienced together by both women and men.

Bibliography

Arias, Rosario. "'All the World's a Stage': Theatricality, Spectacle and the 'Flâneuse' in Doris Lessing's Vision of London.' *Journal of Gender Studies* 14.1 (March 2005): 3-11. Print.

Bastida López, Patricia. 'On Women, Christianity, and History: An Interview with Michèle Roberts.' *Atlantis. Revista de la Asociación Española de Estudios Anglo-Americanos* 25.1 (2003): 93-107. Print.

Bastida, Patricia. 'Bilingüismo y biculturalismo en la narrativa de Michèle Roberts.' *UNED*. Web. 28 April 2010. <http://www.uned.es/cagijon/web/activida/publica/entemu01/a8.PDF>.

Bishop, Edward. *Modern Novelists: Virginia Woolf*. London: Macmillan, 1991. Print.

Blanton, Casey. *Travel Writing: The Self and the World. Studies in Literary Themes and Genres*. New York: Simon & Schuster Macmillan, 1997. Print.

Booth, Alison. 'Recovery 2.0: Beginning the Collective Biographies of Women Project.' *Tulsa Studies in Women's Literature* 28.1 (Spring 2009): 15-36. Print.

Brontë, Charlotte. *Jane Eyre*. London: Penguin, 1847. Print.

Buss, Helen M. *Repossessing the World: Reading Memoirs by Contemporary Women*. Toronto: Wilfrid Laurier UP, 2002. Print.

Butler, Judith. 'Subjects of Sex, Gender and Desire: Women as the Subject of Feminism.' *Gender Trouble, Feminism and the Subversion of Identity*. London: Routledge, 1990. Print.

Butler, Tim and Chris Hamnett. 'Walking Backwards to the Future Waking Up to Class and Gentrification in London.' *Urban Policy and Research* 27.3 (2009): 217-228. Print.

Byrin, Kristine A. *Women, Revolution, and Autobiographical Writing in the Twentieth Century: Writing History, Writing the Self.* New York: The Edwin Mellen Press, 2007. Print.

Carter, Angela. *The Bloody Chamber.* London: Penguin, 1981. Print.

---. *The Sadeian Woman: An Exercise in Cultural History.* London: Virago, 1979. Print.

Castaneda, Terri. 'American Indian Lives and Voices: The Promise and Problematics of Life Narratives.' *Reviews in Anthropology* 38.2 (April 2009): 132-165. Print.

Ciplijauskaité, Biruté. *La Novela Femenina Contemporánea (1970 1985) Hacia una Tipología de la Narración en Primera Persona.* Barcelona: Anthropos, 1988.

Cixous, Hélène. 1975. 'Sorties.' *New French Feminisms: An Anthology.* Ed. Elaine Marks and Isabelle de Courtivron. London: Harvester Wheatsheaf, 1980: 231-235. Print.

Cixous, Hélène, Keith Cohen and Paula Cohen. 'The Laugh of the Medusa.' *Signs* 1.4 (Spring 1976): 875-893. Print.

Davies, Brian. *The Thought of Thomas Aquinas.* New York: Oxford UP, 1992.

Dunn, Sara, Blake Morrison and Michèle Roberts, eds. *Mind Readings: Writers' Journeys through Mental States.* London: Minerva, 1996. Print.

Falcus, Sarah. *Michèle Roberts: Myths, Mothers and Memories.* Bern: Peter Lang AG, 2007. Print.

Fish, Tom with Jennifer Perkins. *The Literary Criticism Web.* 1999. Web. 15 June 2009. <http://english.ucumberlands.edu/litcritweb/theory/feminist.htm>.

Fitzgerald, Thomas K. *Metaphors of Identity: A Culture Communication Dialogue.* New York, Albany: State University of New York Press, 1993. Print.

Fitzpatrick, Sean, ed. *Reflections on Psychology, Culture and Life: The Jung Page.* Web. 20 May 2009. <http://www.cgjungpage.org>.

Galván, Fernando. 'Writing as a Woman: A Conversation with Michèle Roberts.' *EJES: European Journal of English Studies* 2.3 (1998): 359-375. Print.

García-Sánchez. María Soraya. 'A Conversation with Michèle Roberts about Novels, History and Autobiography.' *Journal of International Women's Studies* 12.1 (January 2011). Web.

---. 'Talking about Women, History, and Writing with Michèle Roberts.' *Atlantis: Revista de la Asociación Española de Estudios Anglo-Americanos* 27. 2 (December 2005): 137-47. Print.

Gilbert, Sandra M. and Susan Gubar. *The Madwoman in the Attic: The Woman Writer and the Nineteenth-Century Literary Imagination.* New Haven: Yale UP, 1984.

Head, Thomas. *Medieval Hagiography: An Anthology.* New York: Routledge, 2001. Print.

Hoesterey, Ingeborg. *Pastiche: Cultural Memory in Art, Film, Literature.* Bloomington: Indiana UP, 2001. Print.

Husain, Shahrukh. *La Diosa.* Colonia: Taschen GmbH, 2001. Print.

Jong, Erica. *What do Women Want? Power, Sex, Bread & Roses.* London: Bloomsbury, 1999. Print.

Jung, Carl Gustav and R. Wilhelm. *El Secreto de la Flor de Oro.* Barcelona: Piados, 1996. Print.

Jusino, Ramon K. 'Mary Magdalene: Author of the Fourth Gospel?' 1998. Web. 12 April 2009. <http://www.BelovedDisciple.org>.

King, Nicola. *Memory, Narrative, Identity: Remembering the Self.* Edinburgh: Edinburgh UP, 2000. Print.

Kristeva, Julia. 'Woman Can Never Be Defined.' *New French Feminisms: An Anthology.* Ed. Elaine Marks and Isabelle de Courtivron. New York: Schocken Books, 1980: 137-8. Print.

Knoppers, Laura Lunger, ed. *The Cambridge Companion to Early Modern Women's Writing.* Cambridge: Cambridge UP, 2009. Print.

Lane, Maggie. *Literary Daughters.* London: Robert Hale, 1989. Print.

Lessing, Doris. *The Golden Notebook.* London: Harper Perennial Modern Classics, 2007 (1962). Print.

Liseux, Thérèse of. *Story of a Soul: The Autobiography of St. Thérèse of Liseux.* Institute of Carmelite St.: ICS Publications, 1996. Print.

Magezis, Joy. *Teach Yourself Women's Studies.* London: Hodder Headline, 1996. Print.

Miller, Lucasta. *The Brontë Myth.* London: Vintage, 2002. Print.

Milner, Marion. *A Life of One's Own*. London: Routledge, 2010. Print.
---. *Eternity's Sunrise: A Way of Keeping a Diary*. London: Routledge, 2010. Print.
---. *On not Being Able to Paint*. London: Routledge, 2010. Print.
Moore, Katharine. *She for God. Aspects of Women and Christianity*. London: Allison and Busby, 1978. Print.
Morris, Pam. *Literature and Feminism*. Oxford: Blackwell, 1993. Print.
Morrison, Toni. *Beloved*. London: Picador, 1987. Print.
Murdock, Maureen. *Ser mujer: un viaje heroico, un apasionante camino hacia la totalidad*. Madrid: Gaia, 1999. Print.
Nichols, Aidan. *Discovering Aquinas: An Introduction to his Life, Work and Influence*. London: Darton, Longman and Todd, 2002. Print.
Parsons, Deborah L. *Streetwalking the Metropolis: Women, the City and Modernity*. Oxford: Oxford UP, 2000. Print.
Pérez Gil, María del Mar. 'La escritura de la identidad en las novelas de Michèle Roberts.' *Mosaicos y Taraceas: Deconstrucción feminista de los discursos de género*. Alcalá: Universidad de Alcalá Servicio de Publicaciones, 2000: 179-196. Print.
---. 'The Search for the Other in Michèle Roberts's *The Wild Girl*.' *Mujer e Identidad, Distintas Voces: Ensayos de Literatura y Traducción*. Las Palmas de Gran Canaria: Chandlon Inn Press, 2000: 149-165. Print.
Pinkola Estés, Clarissa. *Women Who Run with Wolves*. London: Random House, 1993. Print.
Poorthuis, Marcel. 'Eve's Demonic Offspring. A Jewish Motif in German Literature.' *Eve's Children: the Biblical Stories Retold and Interpreted in Jewish and Christian Traditions*. Ed. Gerard P. Luttikhuizen. Leiden: Brill Academic Publishers, 2003: 57-76. Print.
Qualls-Corbert, Nancy. *La Prostituta Sagrada*. Barcelona: Obelisco, 1997. Print.
Raven, Susan and Alison Weir. *Women in History*. London: Weidenfeld and Nicolson, 1981. Print.

Richards, Linda L., ed. 'January Talks to Michèle Roberts.' *January Magazine*. 2001. Web. 26 October 2003. <http://www.januarymagazine.com/profiles/micheleroberts.html>.
Roberts, Michèle. *A Piece of the Night*. London: The Women's Press, 1978. Print.
---. 'Being a Woman'. *BBC World Service*. 2001. Web. 19 September 2004. <http://www.bbc.co.uk/worldservice/arts/features/womenwriters/roberts_being.shtml>.
---. *Daughters of the House*. London: Virago Press, 1992. Print.
---. *Fair Exchange*. London: Little Brown, 1999. Print.
---. *Flesh and Blood*. London: Virago Press, 1994. Print.
---. *Food, Sex & God: On Inspiration and Writing*. London: Virago Press, 1998. Print.
---. *Impossible Saints*. London: Virago Press, 1997. Print.
---. *In the Red Kitchen*. London: Vintage, 1990. Print.
---. 'Michèle Roberts.' *BBC World Service*. 2001. Web. 19 September 2004. <http://www.bbc.co.uk/worldservice/arts/features/womenwriters/roberts_life.shtml>.
---. *Michèle Roberts*. Web. 15 November 2009. <http://www.micheleroberts.co.uk>.
---. *Mother Teresa, a Saint Making Business*. Channel 4. 24 October 2003. Television.
---. *Paper Houses: A Memoir of the '70s and Beyond*. London: Virago Press, 2007. Print.
---. *The Book of Mrs Noah*. London: Vintage, 1987. Print.
---. *The Looking Glass*. London: Little Brown, 2000. Print.
---. *The Mistressclass*. London: Little Brown, 2003. Print.
---. *The Visitation*. London: The Women's Press, 1983. Print.
---. *The Wild Girl*. London: Minerva, 1984. Print.
Roe, Sue et all. *The Semi-Transparent Envelope: Women Writing Feminism and Fiction*. London: Marion Boyars Publishers, 1994. Print.
Showalter, Elaine. *A Literature of Their Own: From Charlotte Brontë to Doris Lessing*. London: Virago Press, 1977. Print.

---. *Inventing Herself: Claiming a Feminist Intellectual Heritage.* London: PanMcMillan, 2001. Print.
Siegel, Kristi. *Women's Autobiographies, Culture, Feminism. Series XXVII Feminist Studies*, vol. 6. New York: Peter Lang Publishing, 1999. Print.
Smith, Jules. 'Michèle Roberts.' *Contemporary Writers: British Council.* 2008. Web. 3 January 2009. <http://www.contemporarywriters.com/authors/?p=auth109>.
Smith, Sidonie. *Subjectivity, Identity, and the Body: Women's Autobiographical Practices in the Twentieth Century.* Bloomington and Indianapolis: Indiana UP, 1993. Print.
Sommer, Doris. "'Not Just a Personal Story': Women's *testimonies* and the Plural Self.' *Life/Lines: Theorizing Women's Autobiography.* New York: Cornell UP, 1988. Print.
Spencer, Jane. *The Rise of the Woman Novelist: From Aphra Behn to Jane Austen.* Oxford: Basil Blackwell, 1986. Print.
Spender, Dale. *Mothers of the Novel: 100 Good Women Writers before Jane Austen.* London: Pandora, 1986. Print.
Staves, Susan. *A Literary History of Women's Writing in Britain, 1660-1789.* Cambridge: Cambridge UP, 2006. Print.
Suranyi, Anna. 'Virile Turks and Maiden Ireland: Gender and National Identity in Early Modern English Travel Literature.' *Gender and History* 21.2 (August 2009): 241-262. Print.
Steinem, Gloria. *Outrageous Acts and Everyday Rebellions.* London: Jonathan Cape, 1984. Print.
Villegas López, Sonia. *Mujer y religión en la narrativa anglófona contemporánea.* Huelva: Universidad de Huelva, 1999.
---. 'Telling Women's Lives: Vision as Historical Revision in the Work of Michèle Roberts.' *Atlantis. Revista de la Asociación Española de Estudios Anglo-Norteamericanos* 23.1 (2001): 173-188. Print.
Voss, Norrine. "'Saying the Unsayable': An Introduction to Women's Autobiography.' *Gender Studies: New Directions in Feminist Criticism.* Ed. Judith Spector. Bowling Green State University Press, 1986: 218-223. Print.

Walker, Nancy A. *Feminist Alternatives: Irony and Fantasy in the Contemporary Novel by Women*. Jackson: University Press of Mississippi, 1990. Print.
Walker, Natasha. *The New Feminism*. London: Little Brown, 1998. Print.
Waugh, Patricia. 1992. 'Modernism, Postmodernism, Gender: The View from Feminism.' *Feminisms*. Eds. Sandra Kemp and Judith Squires. Oxford: Oxford UP, 1997: 206-210. Print.
Weldon, Fay. *The Life and Loves of a She-Devil*. London: Hodder and Stoughton, 1983.
Whitworth, Michael H., ed. *Modernism*. Oxford: Blackwell Publishing, 2007. Print.
Wilson, Cheril A. 'Placing the Margins: Literary Reviews, Pedagogical Practices, and the Canon of Victorian Women's Writing.' *Tulsa Studies in Women's Literature* 28.1 (Spring 2009): 57-74. Print.
Wolf, Janet. *Feminine Sentences: Essays on Women and Culture*. Cambridge: Polity Press, 1990. Print.
---. 'The Invisible Flâneuse. Women and the Literature of Modernity.' *Theory Culture Society* 2 (1985): 37-46. Print.
Woodman, Marion. 'La feminidad consciente: madre, virgin, anciana.' *Ser Mujer*. Ed. Connie Zweig. Barcelona: Kairós, 1999: 113-121. Print.
Woolf, Virginia. *Killing the Angel in the House: Seven Essays*. Harmondsworth: Penguin, 1995. Print.
---. *Moments of Being*. Ed. Jeanne Schulkind. New York: Harcourt Brace & Company, 1985. Print.
---. *To the Lighthouse*. Boston: Mariner Books, 1989. Print.

www.ingramcontent.com/pod-product-compliance
Lightning Source LLC
LaVergne TN
LVHW012020060526
838201LV00061B/4392